# iPad®
# MADE EASY

This is a FLAME TREE book
First published 2013

**Publisher and Creative Director**: Nick Wells
**Project Editor**: Polly Prior
**Art Director**: Mike Spender
**Layout Design**: Jane Ashley
**Copy Editor**: Daniela Nava
**Technical Editor**: Mark Mayne
**Screenshots**: Roger Laing
Thanks to: Laura Bulbeck, Esme Chapman, Emma Chafer, Stephen Feather and Karen Fitzpatrick

This edition published 2013 by
**FLAME TREE PUBLISHING**
6 Melbray Mews
Fulham, London SW6 3NS
United Kingdom

www.flametreepublishing.com

15 17 16
13 15 17 19 20 18 16 14 12

ISBN 978-0-85775-622-0

A CIP record for this book is available from the British Library upon request.

Printed in China

All non-screenshot pictures are courtesy of © 2013 Apple Inc.: 3, 8, 9, 20, 26, 88, 118, 241; cloudbite.co.uk: 101; gadgetmix.com: 24; griffintechnology.com: 22; JBL: 239; Kensington.com: 242; Logitech: 240; Padfoot: 238; Paper Nomad: 237 and Shutterstock and © the following photographers: baranq: 7, 184; Denphumi: 5, 54; l i g h t p o e t : 6, 128; Mihai Simonia: 7, 216; 1000 Words: 5, 86; Rido/Shutterstock: 4, 14; robert_s : 12; wavebreakmedia : 6, 150. Other images courtesy of Flame Tree Publishing Ltd

# iPad®
## MADE EASY

ROGER LAING

**FLAME TREE
PUBLISHING**

# CONTENTS

Time to get familiar with the iPad, its controls, all the essential apps you'll need and the everyday tasks that you'll use it for. Starting with the basics, you will learn all about the iPad's anatomy and the whereabouts of different buttons, as well as understanding what goes on inside your device. This chapter also takes you through other essentials such as using the App Store and syncing.

## GETTING CONNECTED . . . . . . . . . . . . . . . . . . . . . 54

The iPad is the whole world at your fingertips. In this chapter you'll learn how to browse the internet, send and receive messages and emails, use video calling, and master social media channels such as Facebook and Twitter. Getting connected doesn't end there; you'll also get to grips with how to make the most of the iPad's location services.

## PHOTOGRAPHS & VIDEO . . . . . . . . . . . . . . . . . . . 86

With its high quality Camera and Video apps, the iPad is the perfect tool when it comes to capturing, viewing and storing great photos and movies. Featuring step by step guides to taking, editing, and sharing photos and videos, this chapter will leave you feeling like a fully competent iPad photographer. In addition you'll learn how to rent and buy videos through the iTunes store, and view them using Apple TV.

The iPad is the perfect device for browsing, downloading, arranging and reading books and magazines via the iBooks and Newsstand apps – and this chapter shows you exactly how to do so. What's more this chapter introduces other reading apps such as Kindle and Zinio, and details how to adjust the appearance of text to ensure that you get the best reading experience possible.

When it comes to finding a comprehensive entertainment device, the iPad is king. This chapter describes how the iTunes, Podcast and Music apps allow you to use your iPad to browse, create and edit playlists and to make and share your own music. In addition you'll learn all about gaming on your iPad and discover apps that complement every aspect of your lifestyle, from shopping to cooking.

# WORKING

From built in apps such as Notes, to Documents and Keynote which can be downloaded from the app store, the iPad is your hub for work as well as play. This chapter will talk you through these incredibly useful apps, together with iWork, Numbers, Google Docs and Draw. You will also learn how to print from your iPad and keep in the loop by using Calendar to schedule meetings and Contacts to stay in touch.

# ADVANCED iPAD

Once you're comfortable with your iPad and know how to use it, it's time to really make it your own. This chapter tells you how to customize the way different apps and controls work. Amongst other things you will also learn how to troubleshoot issues such as connectivity and power loss, as well as introducing the various ways in which you can accessorize your iPad to optimum effect.

# INTRODUCTION

Loved, desired and applauded since it was first launched, the iPad has revolutionized personal computing. Forget your laptop, ditch the desktop PC: the iPad is rapidly becoming the essential accessory for managing everyday life.

**Above:** The iPad with Retina display has incredible screen clarity and is the fastest version yet.

## YOUR WORLD AT YOUR FINGERTIPS

The iPad is far more than a gadget. Once you have one it is almost impossible to remember life without it. Never before has there been a device that makes it this simple to read books, newspapers and magazines, browse the web, go shopping, play games, see movies, watch TV, listen to music, share photos, research ideas for business, write a report and organize the day. What's more, you can do all this and still communicate via email or chat with friends, family and work colleagues, whether close to home or across continents. With the iPad, your world is in your hand.

## EVERYTHING YOU NEED TO KNOW

Apple is renowned for the simple elegance of their design. Following the principles set by their founder – the late Steve Jobs – they want to create technology that just works. While the iPad is user friendly, there is so much that it does that is not immediately obvious.

This book is designed to help you get the most from your iPad. It will guide you through the myriad ways you can use the iPad for both personal and business use. Like the iPad, we'll aim to make things simple and clear. Where it is unavoidable to use technical terms we will explain exactly what they mean.

## Different Generations, Similar Features

Amazingly, since it first appeared in 2010, Apple has launched five different models of iPad, each with two options available – Wi-Fi only and Wi-Fi plus Cellular.

**Above:** The iPad home screen displays all your apps simply and clearly.

Unfortunately, the naming of each model has been quite confusing. The original iPad was clear and so was iPad 2. But that was followed not by iPad 3 but the New iPad featuring the super-high-resolution Retina display, which Apple dubbed 'Resolutionary'. The new iPad was itself replaced within six months by a faster version referred to as iPad with Retina display. In addition, there's a smaller iPad named iPad mini.

To clarify it for themselves, Apple refer to each new version as a generation, even though its lifespan is fairly short. So in this book we'll refer to the first, second, third and fourth generation iPads (or iPad 1, iPad 2, iPad 3, iPad 4 for short) plus the iPad mini.

While there are physical differences between the generations – for

**Above:** The iPad mini is a smaller version of the iPad.

example, iPad 4 has a more powerful processor than the others, and the original iPad has no camera – many features are controlled by the operating system (iOS).

The latest iOS runs on all iPads, with the exception of the original iPad, but that still supports most features mentioned in this book. Where features are available only on specific models, this will be noted in the text.

## SHORT SECTIONS

Pick up your iPad and flick through the screens and you'll often come across something new. Similarly, this book is not designed to be read in one sitting but to be a handy guide. For example, the section on gestures can be read on its own and you can practise them on your iPad until you feel confident that you can use them correctly. At the same time, it is a useful reference, if you need to remind yourself of some of the more advanced gestures later on.

## STEP-BY-STEP

Throughout this book you'll find there are many step-by-step guides that take you through the precise actions you need to follow on certain tasks. This may be anything from connecting to your wireless network, setting up email or editing your photos to creating a new playlist for your music or troubleshooting app problems. Each step-by-step guide has clear, concise instructions on what to do and also explains any differences between the various iPad versions, so you can be sure you won't miss out.

## HELP!

In the unlikely event you do get really stuck on a particular topic, we're here to help. Simply email your query to Flame Tree Publishing at *support@flametreepublishing.com*. While we cannot operate a 24-hour helpline for any iPad questions, we will respond by email as soon as possible.

## YOUR GUIDE

If this is your first iPad, this book is designed to get you up and running as quickly as possible. There's plenty too for the more experienced user to discover. The author Roger Laing delves into some of the more advanced features and uses his experience as a technology writer to explain briefly and clearly how they improve your iPad experience and add to the fun.

**Above:** Editing photos is just one of the ways you can use your iPad.

## DO MORE

Everyone has their own opinion on what's best about the iPad. It may be watching a movie or TV programme on a display that can vie with the best of screens. It could be playing

**Above:** It is easy to use your iPad to watch films and TV programmes on websites such as BBC iPlayer.

games with a speed and power that rivals any console. It may be having a photo gallery to share with family and friends or the incredible range of apps, many of which have the potential to change the way you live and work. The good thing is you don't have to choose between any of these. The iPad has them all and more. This book will get you started; after that the possibilities are virtually unlimited.

## SEVEN CHAPTERS

The contents of this book are split into eight chapters. Chapter one will show you how to get started with the iPad itself, the hundreds of thousands of apps available and how to stay up-to-date. Chapter two covers getting connected with email, video calling, social media and the like. Chapter three is all about photos and video – taking photos if you have an iPad with a camera, editing them to add stunning effects, as well as viewing, storing and sharing them. It also offers practical advice on taking, viewing and editing your own videos, as well as buying and renting movies, and TV shows, etc. Chapter four is where to read all about the books, newspapers and magazines that turn your iPad into a digital reader.

**Left:** Keep up to date on current affairs by reading news articles on your iPad.

Chapter five is the entertainment channel, where you can discover how to listen, store and even make your own music or enter another world with games. Chapter six shows that the iPad is also a good work tool, which can help you organize your documents, your time, your contacts – in fact as much of your life as you allow. Chapter seven looks at the more advanced features that keep your iPad running smoothly – from customizing and setting your preferences to troubleshooting and security.

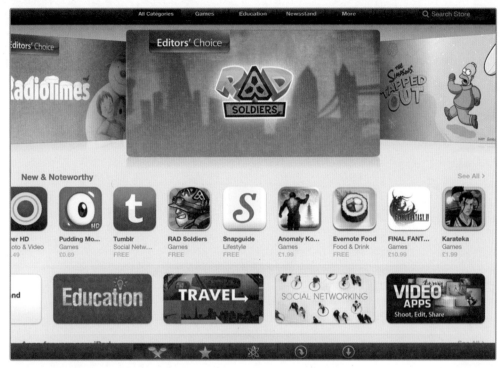

**Above:** Head to the App Store to browse and download apps and get the most out of your iPad.

## HOT TIPS AND SHORT CUTS

Look out, throughout the book, for the Hot Tips, which provide quick and handy information on the way to get the best from your iPad. They also highlight many short cuts and quick techniques to help you become an expert iPad user.

## APPTASTIC

Here in one handy list are the 100 essential apps that no iPad user will want to be without. They are linked to the relevant section in the book, so it's easy to refer back and get more information on the category they cover.

GETTING STARTED

# WHAT IS AN iPAD?

Think of your iPad as the ultimate portable computer – light enough to take wherever you go, yet powerful and versatile enough to do whatever you need.

## TABLET COMPUTER

The arrival of the iPad established the popularity of tablet computers, a type of mobile computer that typically has a touch screen rather than a normal keyboard. Previously, several computer manufacturers had launched tablets but they failed to take off. Apple succeeded because they believed the tablet, which is bigger than a smartphone but smaller than a laptop, had to be better than either at key tasks – such as displaying text and video, organizing your work life and brightening up your personal life.

## YOUR ENTERTAINMENT CENTRE

Whether it's a long read, listening to your favourite music, playing a game with friends around the world or sharing a memory of good times with your photos, the iPad does it all.

### Books and Periodicals

Your portable library, the iPad is an ebook reader which can store hundreds of texts inside and also

**Above:** Download, store and read hundreds of book and magazine texts on your iPad.

## Hot Tip

The small software programs that run on the iPad are called apps (mini-applications). Apple has approved more than a million apps for download through the App Store.

**Above:** Use the touch screen controls in the iPad video app to view high definition music videos in full screen mode.

lets you buy more using the device itself. Apple has one app, iBooks, for reading and storing books, while another app, Newsstand, lets you subscribe to newspapers and magazines. With many other apps from bookstores and publishers, such as Amazon, you literally have access to millions of book titles worldwide and hundreds of periodicals.

### Video

As video viewing is a key feature of the iPad, it comes with its own app. Click on the Videos icon and you can choose between viewing movies, TV shows or music videos, or go to the online store to see what's available to purchase.

Once you've started the video player, using the touch screen controls, you can view the video full screen for uninterrupted viewing. Not surprisingly, the app takes full advantage of the super clear Retina display (iPad 3 and 4 only) and can playback full HD video.

### Music

Previously, the music app was named the iPod; now it takes full advantage of the iPad's larger screen and is more like iTunes that runs on your computer. The artists, for example, and their various album covers are shown on a grid. Select one and you can see all the tracks and associated album covers that you have by that artist.

## Games

Games are another area where the iPad
scores over the smaller screen iPhone.
There are many games specially developed
for the iPad, which has the speed and
power to match the graphics of traditional
games consoles. If you want to rank
your scores against friends and family,
sign up for an account on the iPad's
Game Center app.

**Above:** Photos organizes your images in albums, displaying them
as stacks of photos, such as My Photo Stream here.

## Photos

Open the Photos app and see all the digital photos stored on the iPad. These can be photos
you've taken with the camera (on all iPads except iPad 1) or transferred via iTunes, a camera
connection or wirelessly. Flick through your pictures by swiping your finger across the screen.

Your albums are shown as stacks of
photos and a new feature, Photo Stream,
keeps all your snaps up-to-date across all
your Apple devices. Three other tabs
show photos that have been tagged with
names (Faces), have details of where
they were taken (Places) or are grouped
according to when the pictures were
shot (Events).

## Hot Tip

Don't worry if the Faces, Places
or Events tabs are missing in
Photos. It simply means that
none of your photos have been
tagged that way.

# YOUR BUSINESS RESEARCH ASSISTANT

The iPad is a wonderful research tool that can help you find the important information you
need, take notes or even full reports and share them afterwards.

## Web Content

With Safari for iPad you have a browser that is similar
to any you have used on a computer. It gives you
access to all the same research sources – from Google
search to Wikipedia and millions in between. With
support for tabbed browsing, it's now easy to move
backwards and forwards between the different pages
you have visited.

**Hot Tip**

To check the exact address
where a link on a web page
will take you, press and
hold the link.

## Making and Storing Notes

Nothing is worse than having an idea you want to make a note of and no way to write it
down. Fortunately, the iPad comes with its own Notes app. There's space on the yellow ruled
notepad to jot down ideas, plan a project and write down a meeting report. For writing a To
Do list, the better option is the iPad's new list writing app, called Reminders. This lets you
create a task list – from the weekly shop to packing for a holiday – for which you can set a
reminder that will alert you when it
needs to be done.

## Sharing Information

Your notes and reminders can be synced
with your other Apple devices, so you
always have access to the latest version.
You can also share your reminders with
others through iCloud. Similarly, there are
many file sharing services – from
Dropbox to Evernote and Google Docs –
which enable you to collaborate and
work on documents with friends and
colleagues, wherever they are, direct
from your iPad.

**Above:** Reminders allows you to make lists and set timed reminders.
Sync your reminders with other Apple devices and share over iCloud to
keep all relevant people updated, wherever they may be.

# ANATOMY OF AN iPAD

While there are few obvious physical differences between iPads, there are some subtle and not so subtle variations between each generation. Here's your guide to the physical layout of the iPad.

## FRONT

**①** Headphone Socket

The 3.5 mm audio jack point works fine with headphones or earbuds you use with other Apple devices, such as the iPhone or iPod Touch, but others may need an inexpensive adapter to fit.

**②** Sleep/Wake Button

Also known as the On/Off button.

○ **Sleep mode**: press this button once and this will put your iPad to sleep. You can still play music but the screen will be off. To wake the iPad instantly and start using it, press the Sleep/Wake button once (or the Home button) and swipe across the slide to unlock button.

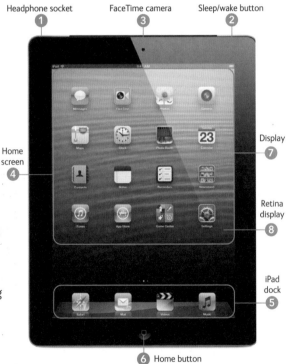

Headphone socket ①    FaceTime camera ③    Sleep/wake button ②

Home screen ④

Display ⑦

Retina display ⑧

iPad dock ⑤

⑥ Home button

○ **Shutdown**: turns the iPad off completely, saving your battery. To switch off, press and hold the Sleep/Wake button for a few seconds. Confirm your decision by using the slide to power off button to shut down.

### ❸ FaceTime Camera

As its name suggests, it is mainly meant for using with FaceTime video chat, so other people can see you. On the iPad 2 and 3, the camera provides VGA-quality video as well as 0.3 megapixel stills. This has been upgraded on the iPad 4 and mini to be FaceTime HD and support 1.2-megapixel stills and 720 mp video.

### ❹ Home Screen

The Home screen has the app icons that you tap to run the app. Swipe right on the Home screen and you'll flip through the different pages of apps you have available. You can also organize your apps into folders. To do so, just press on an app icon until it starts shaking and then drag it on top of the icon you want to share the folder. A folder is automatically created, which you can rename. Tap on the folder and you can access the apps inside.

### ❺ iPad Dock

This dock bar appears at the foot of the Home screen and stays in place as you scroll between the pages. It means these apps are always available from any Home screen page. As a result you will want the apps you use most frequently to be in the dock. By default, the Safari, Mail, Photos and Music apps will be there, but you can customize the dock to include six apps of your choice. To add an app, press and hold until it begins to shake, then drag it to the dock. To make room for a different app, if you already have six in the dock, press and hold one of the apps then drag it to the Home screen.

### ❻ Home Button

The only physical button on the front of your iPad. When you are in one app – such as Safari or Mail – press this once to return to the main Home screen page and launch another app. Pressing it twice reveals the icons of apps that have recently been running.

## Hot Tip

One way to help preserve battery life is to set your screen to Auto-Lock when you're not using it. To do so, tap the Settings icon, select General, then Auto-Lock and set the interval to the time you prefer.

**7** Display: iPad 1, 2 and Mini (*see previous page*)

The screen of the iPad 1 and 2 is 9.7 inches when measured diagonally. With a resolution of 1024x768 pixels that means it packs 132 pixels per inch. The iPad mini shares the same resolution as its bigger siblings, but with a smaller display – at 7.9 inches measured across the diagonal – it has more pixels per inch (163 vs 132). The result is slightly clearer detail. On both screens, the backlit multi-touch display has a special coating to help prevent smearing and smudges from greasy fingerprints.

**8** Retina Display: iPad 3 and 4 (*see previous page*)

With 3.1 million pixels packed in to the same 9.7-inch screen as earlier iPads, the Retina displays on the iPad 3 and 4 have more pixels for their size than the current generation of high-definition television (HDTV). As a result they can play movies in full HD. In fact, everything from video to photos and text is sharper and more detailed. They can display still images in stunning detail up to 19 megapixels. The name Retina comes from the fact that with a pixel density of 264 pixels per inch (PPI), the pixels are too closely packed together for the average human eye to discern between them.

① iSight camera

⑥ Side switch

② SIM card slot

⑤ Volume buttons

iPad

④ Speaker

③ Dock connector

### Touch screen

With no physical keyboard, you control the machine and enter text by tapping and swiping the display.

# REAR

**1** iSight Camera

The initial video camera on the iPad 2 (iPad 1 has no cameras) has been upgraded from a

0.7-megapixel lens that shoots video at 720p to a 5-megapixel lens on later models, which shoots full 1080p HD (high-definition) video. The range of features includes video stabilization, auto-focus, tap to focus, face detection and geotagging.

## ② SIM Card Slot

This holds the micro-SIM card your telecommunications company will give you to access their data networks. The cover is easily removed using the SIM card tool supplied or an ordinary paper clip. The new iPad can connect to the regular 3G or faster 3.5G HSPA+ network and, in countries where they are available, the 4G LTE networks.

## ③ Dock Connector

To much consternation, the original 30-pin dock connector used with iPad 1, 2 and 3 has been changed to the much lighter, smaller Lightning connector on newer models. The dock connector allows you to hook up to your computer, power charger, camera connector and other accessories. As a result of the change many existing accessories will not work with the iPad 4 or mini.

## ④ Speaker

The speaker grill is at the bottom edge of your iPad, so make sure that it is not obscured by the cover you use.

## ⑤ Volume Buttons

With the rocker button, you press one end to turn the sound up and the other to turn it down. As you adjust the setting, a box will appear on screen with a speaker icon and a volume strength bar.

## ⑥ Side Switch

This can do one of two things. By default, it is used to lock the orientation of the iPad, so it stays in either vertical (portrait) or horizontal (landscape) mode. If you go to Settings, you can change it to be a mute switch that turns the iPad's volume off.

> **Hot Tip**
>
> Cleverly, the iPad remembers two volume settings: one for the volume you set when using headphones and the other for the sound level when using the speaker.

# INSIDE THE iPAD

With each new model the iPad has become faster and more capable. Here we look at the main features to help you decide which one is right for you.

**Above:** The iPad unpacked! Complex and sleek, the iPad is also surprisingly environmentally friendly, boasting many eco features, including a recyclable aluminium and glass enclosure.

## Memory (RAM)

As each new generation of iPad does more, so more memory is needed to run the operating system and apps. The initial 256MB of memory was doubled for the iPad 2 (and iPad mini) and doubled again to 1GB for the iPad 3 and 4.

## Processor

Each generation of the iPad has seen an increase in the power of the processor. In particular, iPads 3 and 4 have many more pixels to handle, with the new Retina display, while also having the power to handle voice dictation and beautiful graphics rendering for photos and games. The iPad mini, which doesn't have a Retina display, shares the same spec as the iPad 2.

## Storage Options

However much space you need to store your music, videos and photos, you'll probably end up wanting more. Each generation of the iPad comes in three sizes: 16 GB, 32 GB and 64 GB. Typically, this would allow you to store:

- **16 GB**: 3,000 songs, 10,000 photos, 40 hours of video

- **32 GB**: 6,000 songs, 20,000 photos, 80 hours of video

- **64 GB**: 12,000 songs, 40,000 photos, 160 hours of video.

Rather than carry everything around with you, you can use online storage services, such as Apple's iCloud, for your music, files and apps, downloading them only when you want them. However, that may not always be convenient. Downloads can be costly on 3G and you may not always have Wi-Fi access when you need it.

## Hot Tip

Don't forget to allow for extra storage on the new Retina iPads to accommodate the larger file sizes of HD games and movies and high-resolution (hi-res) photos.

### Wi-Fi/Cellular

All versions of the iPad are available with just Wi-Fi or with Wi-Fi plus Cellular. On the earlier iPads – iPad 1 and 2 – with a SIM card and subscription from a mobile provider, you can use their 3G data networks to surf the web, download apps, get email, etc. No voice services are included on any iPad models, so you can't make a call as you can with the iPhone (except over Wi-Fi through services such as Skype).

### High-speed Cellular

The latest iPad cellular models – iPad 3, 4 and mini – include 4G LTE (4G is the fourth generation of mobile networks: LTE, or Long Term Evolution, is a type of 4G technology). Currently, 4G coverage varies, but most countries have plans to roll out the technology, or a version of it, over the next couple of years. Check with your provider if your local version works with the iPad. 4G promises speeds about five times faster than existing 3G services. However, the latest iPads also include support for the faster 3G wireless technologies (such as HSPA+), which offer a download speed that's about three times faster than what you currently get with the iPad 2.

## Bluetooth

Bluetooth, which is wireless technology that lets you swap data quickly over short distances, has also been upgraded on the iPad 3, 4 and mini. Version 4.0 uses less power and will still work with your existing Bluetooth accessories, such as wireless keyboards, photo uploaders, etc. However, you'll only get the full benefit of the energy efficiency it offers if your devices themselves support the new standard.

## Smart Cover

One of the innovations on the iPad 2 carried over to later iPads is the Smart Cover. This clever magnetic system switches your iPad on when you lift the cover and puts it to sleep when you close it.

**Left and below:**
The Smart Cover, as well as waking, sleeping and protecting your iPad, is also a handy stand for reading, watching and typing.

## Battery Life

Despite differences in screen resolution and processor power, battery life is much the same across all iPads. That is: 10 hours of power for surfing, movie watching and music listening over Wi-Fi – or 9 hours for the same over a mobile connection.

## Hot Tip

In practice, battery life greatly depends on how you use the iPad. You can help the power to last longer by adjusting screen brightness and reducing, or turning off, notifications, location services and push email.

# iPAD BASICS

Getting started with your iPad is simple and opens up a whole new world of entertainment, communication and fun.

## SET UP YOUR iPAD

When you get your brand new iPad, there's remarkably little in the box: just the iPad, power cord and not much else. There's no manual, which is one reason why this book can help to get your iPad adventures off to the best start.

**Above:** Part of the iPad set up process asks you to select the language you want to use.

### Step-by-step

With earlier iPads you had to connect your iPad to your computer – and iTunes – to start the activation process. Since iOS 5.0 you can get going using Wi-Fi.

1. A brand new iPad comes partly charged, so you can start straight away. Turn it on by pressing the Sleep/Wake button on the top (the Apple logo will appear) and slide the button across to start.

2. Pick the language you want to use, by tapping on it. A blue tick will appear beside it. Tap the blue arrow to continue.

3. Choose your location from the list under the map. Usually, your country will be showing automatically. If not, tap Show More, pick your location and tap Next.

**Step 3:** Choose your location by selecting the country you live in from the list under the map.

4.  Next, you'll be asked to connect to your Wi-Fi network. A list will open of those available. A lock beside a name shows it is secured and you will need a password to use it. Tap on your chosen network name. Alternatively, you can use your mobile connection.

5.  You may want to share your location through mapping and social media apps. To do so, you'll have to turn Location Services on. Tap Enable Location Services here and then tap Next.

6.  The usual terms and conditions appear for you to agree before you can proceed.

**Step 5:** Turn on Location Services to share your location through mapping and social media apps.

**Step 6:** Choose whether you want to set up your device as a new iPad or transfer data from an old iPad.

7.  Now, it's time to activate your iPad. If this is your first iPad, select Set Up as New iPad and click the Next button in the top right hand corner. If you are transferring your data from a previous iPad, select one of the other options to transfer from iCloud or iTunes.

**Step 8:** Set up an Apple ID, or sign in with an existing Apple ID, so that you can download apps from App Store and access iTunes.

8.  To get the most from your iPad, you need an Apple ID, which is also used to set up your iTunes account. Click Sign In with an Apple ID if you already have one. Otherwise, Create a Free Apple ID takes you through the process.

9.  Apple then offers to turn on various features. Among them are iCloud, using iCloud for backup, and activating Find My iPad in case you lose your tablet.

10. A list of the phone numbers and email addresses on which you can be contacted via iMessage and FaceTime are shown. You can also set up Siri (on iPad 3, 4 and mini) as your voice activated personal assistant. Go through a few more screens, including registration of your new iPad, and press the final button to Start Using iPad.

**Step 9:** iCloud is an extremely useful way of storing, backing up and sharing data across different devices.

## Hot Tip

If you are unsure, during setup, whether you want to activate any services offered, follow the link at the bottom of the screen, which explains more about them.

### Mobile Connections

If you have a cellular iPad, you will need to install the SIM card, provided separately by the mobile network company. Simply open the SIM card holder on the side of the iPad – using the pin provided – and put in the SIM card. Turn the iPad on and tap the Settings icon then Cellular Data and check this is set to On.

**Step 10:** Once all the set-up steps are complete, press the Start Using iPad button to begin the fun!

## Wi-Fi

All models can use Wi-Fi. Increasingly, hotels, cafés, restaurants, airports, railway stations and the like offer free Wi-Fi. There are also networks of public hotspots – Wi-Fi access points – where you can connect. Some are subscription based, others are free. To connect, tap the Settings icon on the Home screen. Tap Wi-Fi and then On. Under Choose a Network you'll see a list of those available. The signal strength is shown by the number of bars on the wireless symbol. The lock shows that it is a secure network and needs a password to access it. Tap the one you want to use to activate it.

**Above:** To activate a Wi-Fi connection choose a network from the list and enter the password.

## Notifications

While it's good to know what's going on and needs your attention, previous versions of Notifications were distracting. Now you decide when – or if – notifications appear.

### Access the Notification Centre

○ Put your finger on the **black bar** at the top of the screen and swipe it down. The **Notification Center** slides into view, showing what requires attention.

○ Tap **individual items** in the **Notification Center** to switch to the app that created them.

○ Notifications can also appear on your iPad's **Lock screen**. Slide your finger on the notification and it will **unlock the iPad** and go to the **relevant app**.

○ You can **select** which apps send notifications and the order in which they're displayed by **tweaking your settings**:

Hot Tip

If notifications show on your Lock screen they could be seen by anyone passing by. Change this by tapping the Settings icon, then Notifications and sliding the View in Lock Screen button to Off.

1. Tap the **Settings icon** on the Home screen and select **Notifications**.

**Above:** By tapping the Settings icon on the Home screen and selecting Notifications, you can rearrange the order in which you receive notifications and edit which apps you wish to receive them for.

2. Tap **Edit** and then use the three-line handles to move the apps up and down to reflect the order you want for the notifications. Select **Done** when you've finished.

3. Tap on the **arrow** beside any of the apps and choose whether you want them in the Notification Center by sliding the button to **On** or **Off**. You can also select the type of **alert** used.

## Bluetooth

There are several wireless accessories that enhance your iPad – such as an external speaker or wireless headset – most of which connect via Bluetooth.

○ Tap the **Settings icon** then **General**. Tap **Bluetooth** and then switch to **On**.

○ Under **Devices** is a list of nearby **Bluetooth devices**. To connect they must be **paired** with your iPad. **Select** the device – such as a Bluetooth Wireless Keyboard – and type the numbers shown, then press **Enter** to connect.

## Print

While the iPad saves paper, as you can carry all your documents electronically, there are times when you do need to print something out – whether it's a business report or directions to Great Aunt Maisie's house.

**Above:** You can turn on Bluetooth within the Settings app to pair your iPad with wireless accessories such as a wireless keyboard.

⊙ Built in to the iPad is support for printing wirelessly to **AirPrint-enabled printers**, of which there are an increasing number. All that's necessary is for the printer to be on the **same wireless network** as the iPad. You can **print direct** to AirPrint-enabled printers from built-in iPad apps such as Mail, Photos, Safari, Notes and Maps.

⊙ To print a document within an app, tap the arrow icon then **Print**. Press **Select Printer** and choose one from the list. Set the printer options (these are generally fairly limited and differ between apps) and tap **Print**.

⊙ If you don't have an AirPrint-friendly printer, all is not lost. There are **third-party apps**, such as **Printopia** (Mac only) or **Fingerprint** (Mac or Windows) that turn your computer into a print server and will let you print from your iPad or iPhone.

⊙ There are also apps, such as **PrintCentral** (Mac or Windows) for printing from your iPad to any wireless printer, provided it is on the **same** Wi-Fi network. They also connect to printers attached to your computer.

## Search

You know the exact piece of information you need is on your iPad but can't remember where. Search will hunt through all the built-in apps, an individual app or all apps at once to

## Hot Tip
The icon to the left of a Search result shows which app it is from. Simply tap the item to open.

find it. To access it, press the Home button to return to the Home screen page and flick right. As you start entering text, the search results begin to appear.

**Above:** Search your iPad by typing in the search bar on the Home screen; tap a result to open in its app.

# NAVIGATING YOUR IPAD

The iPad is remarkably simple to use, considering the technical complexity behind it. Here's a handy primer on the gestures to use to speed your way around your iPad.

### Gestures

- **Tap**: The most common gesture, the touch equivalent of the mouse click.

- **Double-tap**: Tap twice in quick succession. Primarily used for zooming in on a web page or section of text.

- **Tap and hold**: Works similarly to the right-click on a mouse. Tap on the screen and hold your finger in place and a small pop-up menu appears. In text, for example, this will give you options for cutting and pasting words or whole sentences.

- **Scroll**: The touch equivalent of using the scroll wheel on a mouse to navigate down a web page quickly. Press your finger lightly on the screen then run it up or down to move through the list or web page. On some apps, such as Contacts or Music, there is an alphabetic

**Above:** Apps such as Contacts and Music display an alphabetic scroll bar on the right hand side. Simply press the letter you want and you will be taken directly to the relevant part of the list.

scrollbar on the side. Press the letter you want and the page will automatically scroll to that part of the list.

⊙ **Flick:** An extension of the scroll, this allows you to work your way through a long list, such as Contacts, more quickly. Press your finger gently on the screen then flick up or down. The faster the flick, the quicker the scroll.

⊙ **Swipe:** Another of the primary navigational aids. Swipe left or right to move through your Home screen pages, your images in Photos or up and down to read text in Safari or Newsstand.

⊙ **Pinch:** To zoom in or to open something put your index finger and thumb together on the screen and slowly move them apart. To zoom out do the reverse. The faster you move your fingers, the quicker the zoom.

**Above:** You can rotate individual pictures in your photo albums by touching two fingers on the screen and making a circular gesture.

⊙ **Rotate:** Turn everything upside down. Just put two fingers on the screen and make a circular gesture clockwise or anti-clockwise.

## Hot Tip
A two-fingered swipe has a different effect in some apps; for example, in Photos it returns you to the thumbnail view of your pictures.

## Status Symbols

Just like your computer's menu bar, the iPad has a number of status icons at the top of the screen that show what's going on. Icons for your mobile and Wi-Fi connections are on the left, with other services on the right.

 **Signal strength**: The more bars, the stronger the network signal in your area. One bar shows little to no service, five bars and all is well.

 **Carrier**: At the end of the signal strength indicator is the name of the mobile data network provider, such as 3 or O2-UK.

 **Wi-Fi strength**: This radar-like symbol shows if you're connected to a Wi-Fi network. The more visible bars, the stronger the reception.

 **Personal hotspot**: The two interlinked circles show that your iPad is sharing its high-speed mobile data connection to link a computer or other device, such as an iPod Touch, to the internet. This feature is available only on iPad 3, 4 and mini.

 **Airplane Mode**: When travelling by air, this switches off any communication systems likely to interfere with the plane's controls and lets you can carry on using other apps, such as reading with iBook or writing a report with Pages. When Airplane Mode is turned on, there's a grey plane icon in the status bar.

> # Hot Tip
> **Airplane mode turns off GPS, Bluetooth and Wi-Fi, so you won't be able to use any apps, such as Mail and Maps, which rely on these features.**

**Above:** Activate Aiplane mode by toggling to On in the Settings menu. Note the plane icon in status bar.

**VPN:** Shows you are using a Virtual Private Network (VPN) as a secure connection across the internet to your office systems.

**Syncing icon:** This rotating circle appears when the iPad is trying to make a connection over your Wi-Fi or Bluetooth network.

**Battery status:** When your battery is charging, this icon shows a small lightning bolt. Beside it the percentage figures show how much battery power is left.

**Location Services:** This arrow appears when an app, such as Maps, is using Location Services.

**Play button:** This triangular icon appears in the status bar if you're playing a music track in iTunes.

**Bluetooth:** This is turned on and is being used by your iPad to pair with another device, such as a wireless keyboard.

**Above:** Set an alarm by scrolling through the numbers wheel until it shows your chosen time.

**Alarm clock:** Get ready for your early morning wake-up; this shows you have set an alarm in the Clock app.

**Do not Disturb:** The moon icon shows that no notifications will appear on screen and that no sounds will be made while your iPad is locked or sleeping. This feature is not available on iPad 1.

**Lock:** The small padlock, appearing where the time used to be, indicates that your iPad is locked.

 **Orientation lock:** Wondering why your apps won't change from portrait to landscape? If this icon is in the status bar, it means that the orientation has been locked. To unlock it, double-press the Home button, swipe to the right and tap on the orientation button, so the lock disappears.

## Multitasking

With multitasking you can switch between tasks without having to close them. You can, for example, be using one app – such as your email – and click a link that then opens another, such as Safari, while having other apps from your Calendar to To Do list open. In fact, when you open a new app, the others are paused to save processor power and battery life.

## Multitasking Bar

The Multitasking Bar has all the apps currently running.

- **To open it:** Double-press on the Home button or use the Swipe Gesture described on the next page to reveal the Multitasking Bar. The main screen fades away and you'll see the icons of the currently running apps.

- **To switch to another app:** Simply tap the icon for it. The current app swoops away behind the new one, which takes its place full screen.

- **To shut down any of the open apps:** Go to the Multitasking Bar and tap-and-hold any icon. This starts jiggling. Tap the red circle with white line – which looks like a No Entry sign – and it is removed from the list.

- **Swipe:** If you swipe all the way to the right when the Multitasking Bar is open and you have a quick way of accessing key iPad controls. There's the orientation lock (or mute

button depending on how the Side
Switch is configured), a slider to adjust
screen brightness plus a volume slider
and other controls for your music.

## Multitasking Gestures

A feature that's unique to the iPad and
not available on other iOS devices,
such as the iPhone or iPod touch, is
Multitasking Gestures. Using four
fingers – and your thumb if you
want – you can pinch and swipe to
move quickly between different apps
and pages.

○ **Home screen pinch**: Place four or five
fingers on screen in any app and bring
them together to close it or return to the
Home screen.

○ **Swipe to reveal Multitasking Bar**:
Open the Multitasking Bar by swiping four
or five fingers upwards. To close it again,
swipe down.

○ **Swipe to switch apps**: Instead of
relying on the Multitasking Bar to move
between apps, simply swipe sideways
with four or five fingers and you'll go to
the next open app.

**Above:** Swipe four or five fingers upwards to reveal the
multitasking bar which allows you to move quickly between
multiple apps and pages.

## Hot Tip

To turn **Multitasking Gestures** on,
tap the **Settings** button on the Home
screen and choose **General**. Scroll
down and you'll see the toggle switch
to turn the feature on.

**Above:** To access the Multitasking function, turn the feature on in
the General area of the Settiings app.

# USING YOUR iPAD

Once you get used to the touchscreen keyboard, it's as quick and easy to use as any conventional computer keyboard. In addition, if you decide you don't want to type, ask Siri to do it for you.

## On-screen Keyboard

What gives you the power to work on the iPad just as efficiently as any laptop is the virtual keyboard. In apps that use it, simply touch the area of the screen where you want to write and the keyboard appears.

## The Way It Works

Unlike most keyboards, the iPad's doesn't type the letter when you press the key, but waits until you lift your finger off. There is a benefit. If you press the wrong key, simply slide your finger to the correct one before taking your finger off.

## Three-in-one Keyboard

The main keyboard just has the letters and basic punctuation, with two shift keys for entering uppercase letters. To enter numbers or some of the less frequently used punctuation marks, tap the key marked .?123 to switch keyboard. To return to the first keyboard, press the ABC key, or to access the third keyboard, which has the least frequently used keys, tap #+=

**Above:** To display numbers and punctuation marks, press the .?123 key on the main keyboard.

## Easy Punctuation

Rather than swap between keyboards, there is a faster way to add punctuation marks. Press and hold the .?123 key and slide to the punctuation you want, then lift your finger off. The punctuation mark will appear and the keyboard will revert back to letters, without you having to press the ABC key.

## Cap That

Although it won't happen very often, there may be times when you need to type in all caps. To do so, double-tap the shift key. It will turn blue to show the caps lock is on. When finished, tap once more to disable caps lock. If this doesn't work, you will need to enable the caps lock. To do so, go to Settings, General then Keyboard and switch Enable Caps Lock to On.

## Hot Tip

To use both hands to type split the keyboard. Put two fingers together in the centre of the keyboard and slide them apart. Reinstate a single keyboard by putting one finger on each side of the keyboard and sliding them together.

## Editing Text

No matter how good your typing is, mistakes will always happen.

○ **To correct your text**: Tap where you want the cursor to appear and press the backspace key (marked with a left-pointing arrow and an X inside).

○ **Magnifier**: It can be fiddly to get the cursor exactly where you want it. To make it easier, tap-and-hold the text until a magnifier appears. Move this around the text and when you find the precise point you want, let go.

○ **To select a word**: Tap the insertion point, and the selection buttons appear. There are options to select that word or all of the document. Double tap a word, and

**Above:** To reveal more of your screen, split the keyboard in two by placing two fingers in the centre and sliding them apart.

it is selected and highlighted in blue with two grab points at either end. Drag these either way to select more text. You can also move them up or down to select whole paragraphs.

○ **Once the text is selected**: option buttons appear for cutting or copying it. The Paste option will replace the highlighted text with the last text cut. Depending on the app used, other features, such as styling or text formatting, may be available.

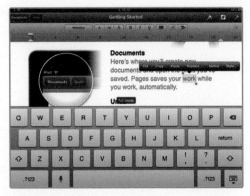

**Above:** Use the magnify tool to highlight a word or selection of words with greater control and precision. Option buttons will be displayed, allowing you to copy, cut and paste as desired.

## Shake It All About

A quick way to delete a message you've written or to undo an edit you've made is to shake your iPad. A dialogue box appears asking if you want to undo the last action or cancel.

## Predictive Text

Rather like someone watching over your shoulder, the iPad will try to be helpful and

**Above:** To stop your iPad from predicting what you want to write toggle Auto-Correction to off in the settings menu.

guess what you're typing. Its suggestions will appear in a text bubble. Press the spacebar or a punctuation mark to accept it. If it's wrong, tap the small x in the text bubble.

The accuracy of the iPad's suggestions should improve the more you type, as it builds up a dictionary of words you commonly use. However, some people do find this feature deeply irritating.

To stop it, go to Settings, General, Keyboard and turn off Auto-Correction.

## Voice Dictation

With the arrival of Siri on iPad 3 and later, you can dictate what you want to write, rather than use the on-screen keyboard to type your text.

1.  Check that voice dictation is turned on. Press the Settings icon, select General, followed by Siri.

2.  You will need to be connected to the internet, either through Wi-Fi or over the mobile network, as dictation is controlled by Siri. This is the voice-commanded personal assistant on your iPad. Everything you say to Siri is sent over the internet to Apple's servers to be interpreted, and the answer or response is then sent back to the iPad.

3.  Open the app you want to use, such as Pages for a document or Mail for email.

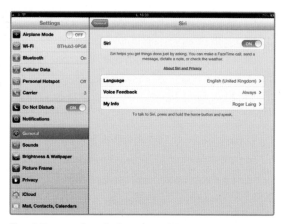

**Step 1:** Turning on Siri in the General area of the Settings menu allows you to dictate what you want to write.

# Hot Tip

**The more you use dictation, the better it gets as it adapts to your accent.**

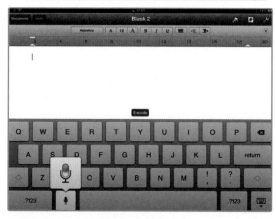

**Step 4:** Touch the microphone icon on the on-screen keyboard to begin dictating your text to Siri.

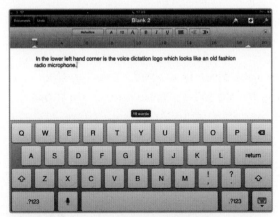

**Step 6**: Tap the microphone key again to view your text.

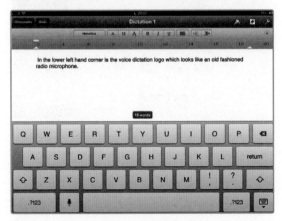

**Step 7**: You can make corrections using the on-screen keyboard.

## Hot Tip

Any app that uses the on-screen keyboard should allow voice dictation, as the feature is built in to the iPad operating system not the program itself.

4. Tap the screen, so the on-screen keyboard appears. In the lower left-hand corner is the voice dictation logo, which looks like an old-fashioned radio microphone.

5. Tap this and start speaking. You will need to include punctuation commands, such as comma, new paragraph, etc. Take care to pronounce special symbols, such as the 'at sign' – @ – seen in emails, clearly.

6. When you've finished dictating, tap the microphone icon again. Your text will appear soon.

7. If you make a mistake, or the dictated text is wrongly transcribed, simply tap where you want to edit and the on-screen keyboard appears. Use this to make your corrections. Siri's done well here – only the end of 'fashioned' has been left off.

8. To add more, repeat the steps.

# APPS

Your iPad comes with just 20 or so apps already loaded, covering the basics from writing notes to playing music. When you want to do more, such as tracking the stars or mind mapping, you can be sure there is an app for it.

## GET AND USE APPS

There's no shortage of apps for your iPad. Currently, there are more than 250,000 free or paid-for apps in the App Store that are specifically designed for the iPad.

### Finding New Apps
You get new apps through Apple's App Store, which is accessed through iTunes on your computer or the App Store app, preloaded on the iPad.

**Above:** When the App Store is open, five useful buttons are displayed on the lower toolbar.

### Apple ID
To use the App Store, you have to be connected to the internet (via Wi-Fi or mobile) and have an Apple ID. You probably entered this when you activated your iPad. If not, go to Settings, iTunes & App Stores (Store on iPad 1) and enter your details or create a new ID.

### Using the App Store App
Accessing the App Store from the iPad itself lets you download new apps directly. Tap the App Store icon to open it and you'll see there are five buttons on the lower toolbar.

○ **Features**: Good for browsing, this screen shows new and noteworthy apps, what's hot and so on. Along the top you can select apps from specific categories, such as games or education.

○ **Charts**: Shows the most popular paid-for and free apps, as well as the top-grossing apps in the store. Scroll down to see more.

○ **Genius**: Press the Turn on Genius button and Apple will recommend new apps for you based on the ones you have already.

**Hot Tip**

In the purchased section, tap Not on This iPad and you'll see all the apps you have bought that have not yet been downloaded to your iPad.

○ **Purchased**: This lists all the apps (both paid-for and free) you have downloaded to any device, such as your computer, using the same Apple ID. If you've deleted an app you want to restore, find it in the list and tap the Cloud icon to download it. You won't have to pay again.

**Above:** Choosing the iPad link in iTunes on your computer allows you to dowload apps and then sync them to your iPad.

○ **Updates**: The badge shows how many updates are available for the apps on your iPad. Click the Update or Update All button to download and install them.

### iTunes

Open iTunes on your computer and click iTunes Store on the top bar, then App Store from the top menu. Click the iPad button at the top of the screen to select that section of the store.

## Choosing Your Apps

There are specially selected lists of new and popular apps. Often these are related to seasonal or topical events, ranging from winter holidays to Halloween and major sporting occasions. To find out more about an app, click its icon to access a dedicated page with details of what it does, screenshots, and customer ratings and reviews. Alternatively, move the mouse over the app icon and click on the small i in the bottom-right corner. The pop-up window that opens will tell you about the app and its features without you having to leave the main page.

## Step-by-step

1. Once you've found the app you can't live without, downloading is quick and easy. On your iPad, tap the icon for the app and the info screen opens.

2. Scroll down to read a description or use the tabs to see ratings and reviews by other customers or related apps from the same developer.

3. Tap the price button and then tap Buy. If it's not a paid-for app, tap the Free button, then Install App.

**Step 1:** Clicking the i in the bottom-right corner of an app icon opens a pop-up iinformation window.

## Hot Tip

**Tap an app to pause download (useful if there are other apps you want to get first). Tap again to resart.**

**Step 2:** The pop-up information window allows you to read ratings and reviews before you decide to download an app.

**Step 4:** Once you have decided to download an app, tap the Buy or Free button and then Install App button.

**Above:** New apps will appear in your homescreen with a 'New' banner across the corner, which remains until the app is opened.

## Downloading Apps from iTunes

Buying an app in iTunes is the same as on the iPad. Select the app and click the price button. This time, though, it is downloaded to your computer. The app is installed on your iPad when you next sync (provided the computer and iPad are both linked to the

4. To stop you buying the same app twice (which did use happen), the button now says Open, Install or Update if you have previously downloaded the app.

5. You may be asked to enter your Apple ID and password. Tap OK when ready.

6. The app's dimmed icon appears on your iPad with a blue progress bar at the bottom. You can move off the page and open other apps while this is happening. Once the download is complete, the app appears on your Home screen, with a New flash across the corner, and is ready to open.

7. If the download is interrupted for any reason, it will re-start automatically the next time you connect to the internet.

### Hot Tip
Sync all your apps to your iPad automatically, no matter where they were originally downloaded. Tap the Settings icon then iTunes & App Stores (Store on iPad 1) and go to the Automatic Downloads section. Slide the switch beside Apps to On.

same Apple ID). Similarly, any apps downloaded to the iPad directly will also be automatically added to iTunes.

## Open and Close Apps

Simply tap the app's icon to open it. To close it and return to the Home screen, just press the Home button. In fact, the app is just suspended. To fully close it, double-press the Home button to open the Multitasking Bar. Press the app's icon and when it starts jiggling, tap the red circle in the corner.

## Arranging Your Apps

With so many apps available, you may soon have several pages of apps. You can rearrange them in two ways – on the iPad and in iTunes.

- ○ **On the iPad**: Tap and hold the icon until it starts jiggling, then drag and drop it where you want it. If you want to move it to the next page of apps, drag it to the edge of the screen. When finished, press the Home button to stop the icons jiggling.

**Above:** Arrange apps on the Home screen of your iPad by tapping and holding an icon until it starts jiggling, and then dragging and dropping to rearrange

- ○ **In iTunes**: Connect your iPad to iTunes, select the iPad from the top bar and then Apps from the top menu. Click and drag the icons where you want them.

## Organizing Apps in Folders

Several related apps can be grouped in folders. Tap and hold the icon of one app and drag it on top of another you wish to group it with. When you lift your finger, a folder will open with both apps inside. The folder is automatically given a name based on the apps included. To change this tap in the box to access the on-screen keyboard. Press the Home button when finished.

To ungroup the apps, tap the folder to open, then tap and hold one of the app's icons until it starts jiggling. Once in Edit mode, drag and drop each app icon out of the folder.

**Above:** Ungroup apps by tapping open a folder, holding an app icon until it jiggles and then dragging apps out the folder.

## Remove Apps

To delete an app, tap and hold its icon, then press the small white X in a white circle that appears in the top-left corner. Be sure you want to do this, as any data entered – such as financial information in an accounts app – will also be permanently removed.

## Running iPhone Apps

Some iPhone apps can work just as well on the iPad. Because they are not specifically designed for the iPad they will usually run in a small window in the middle. You can enlarge the app by tapping the 2x button in the lower-right. If it's blurry or blocky, restore it to its original size by tapping the 1x button.

## Changing App Settings

Most apps keep the options for changing the way they work inside the app itself. Confusingly, though, some apps have a second set of options inside the iPad's Settings app. To access these, tap the Settings icon and select the app from the list on the left. The available options are shown on the right.

### Hot Tip

If you tap and hold an app and the small black X doesn't appear, it means it is one of the default apps, pre-loaded on the iPad. These can't be deleted.

# SYNCING

It's easier than ever to keep your personal information, music, video files and apps on your iPad in sync using iTunes, iCloud or other online cloud services.

## SYNCING WITH ITUNES

As well as keeping all your information up-to-date, syncing is a good safety measure. Each time you sync your iPad with iTunes, a backup is made of all your information. If you lose your iPad or it needs to be reset, you can restore all your data from these backups. It is also the quickest way to transfer large files, such as photos, music or videos.

### Syncing by USB: Step-by-step

1. Connect your iPad to the computer by USB cable. Open iTunes on your computer, and your iPad is listed in the top bar.

**Step 1:** To sync your iPad with your computer connect via USB cable. You can then click the Summary tab and select options to sync contacts, calendars and email accounts.

2. Click the Summary tab and you'll see information about your iPad, along with various options. These include checking for software updates, choosing where you want to back up your data and other general settings, such as automatically opening iTunes when the iPad is connected.

3. Select the Info tab for options to sync your contacts, calendars and email accounts with related Apple apps on the iPad. If you are using iTunes on a PC the available options are more limited.

4. Select the Music tab and check Sync Music. As the iPad has a smaller capacity than your computer, you probably don't want to sync your entire music library. Instead check Selected playlists, artists, albums and genres. Then go through the different categories and check the box beside the ones you want to transfer.

5. Go through the other tabs – Apps, Tones, Movies, TV Shows, Podcasts, Books and Photos – and select what you want to sync. If some of the tabs mentioned aren't visible, don't worry: it just means you have none of that type of content in your iTunes library. When finished, click Apply to start the sync.

## Syncing Wirelessly

Instead of connecting by USB cable to sync, you can use Wi-Fi. Ironically, though, to do so, you first have to connect your iPad with iTunes using a USB cable.

1. Your iPad will show in the top bar in iTunes. Click this and scroll to Options on the Summary tab.

2. Check the box next to Sync with this iPad over Wi-Fi and click Apply in the bottom-right corner.

3. To sync wirelessly, your iPad has to be connected to a power source and be on the same Wi-Fi network as the computer. The computer must also have iTunes open. If you still don't see your iPad in the list of devices, quit and restart iTunes or restart your iPad.

4. Configure your sync options just as you would with the USB connection.

**Hot Tip**

If you check Manually Manage Music and Videos, automatic syncing is turned off. To move songs and movies, first go to the View menu in iTunes and select Show Sidebar. Then drag and drop tracks or clips from your iTunes library onto the iPad icon.

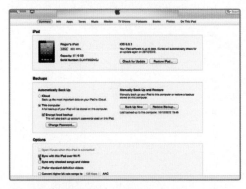

**Above:** Set up wireless sync using iTunes, so that you can sync your devices over Wi-Fi.

# iCLOUD

Apple's online service enables you to keep everything in sync and store your music, photos, documents and apps securely.

## Step-by-step

1.  To set up and configure iCloud: tap Settings then select iCloud. Sign in with your Apple ID and password, or create one if you haven't yet done so.

2.  Choose which iCloud services you want to use: slide the switch to On.

3.  Mail, Contacts, Calendars, Reminders and Notes: these sync with the relevant apps on the iPad.

4.  Safari: this syncs your bookmarks, any open tabs and reading list (that is, web pages you've saved to read later).

5.  Photo Stream: when you take a photo with any iOS device you have, it will be shared and show up in the Photo Stream of the iPad.

6.  Documents & Data: currently works with Apple's office documents, Pages, Numbers and Keynote, but third-party developers can make their apps use it as well.

7.  Find My iPad: help to locate your lost or stolen iPad.

8.  Storage & Backup: sends your data wirelessly to iCloud.

**Step 2**: To choose which iCloud services you want to use, toggle switches to On or Off accordingly.

# ALTERNATIVE CLOUD SERVICES

While iCloud works well with the Mac and iOS devices (iPad, iPhone and iPod touch), not all its features are available to those who don't use Apple software. Fortunately, there are many cloud services that work just as well with the iPad.

## In the Cloud

Cloud services are online storage and syncing facilities. Your content is uploaded – copied – to the company's data centre. Although this is described metaphorically as being 'in the cloud' it is actually in a very down-to-earth city location.

Your stored content can be accessed via the internet, through any browser, or downloaded wirelessly to your computer or iPad, whenever and wherever you want.

## Cloud Apps

Many cloud services have an app for the iPad. Using this, you can access your documents and files stored in the cloud and keep them in sync. Several also have desktop software for your Mac or PC that works in a similar way.

Cloud services you can use direct from your iPad include Google Drive, SkyDrive from Microsoft, Dropbox and Evernote.

Like iCloud, most cloud services offer a free account with a fairly generous amount of storage – typically around 5GB – and paid-for upgrades if more is needed.

**Above:** Evernote for iPad is an example of a cloud service which has an app that you can use to access documents in the cloud.

GETTING CONECTED

# SURFING THE NET

**Through the built-in Safari browser and your Wi-Fi or mobile connection to the internet, you can surf the web, view your favourite sites, update your blog and download files.**

## ACCESS WEBSITES

The high-quality screen makes browsing clear and bright, and with the Retina display on the iPad 3 and 4 the web has never looked so good.

### Browsing

- **Safari** on the iPad is a little different from the one on your **Mac** or **PC**. To open it, **tap** the Safari icon in the dock of commonly used applications at the bottom of the screen.

- When you open Safari, it will show the **last web page** you viewed, if any; otherwise, it will be blank.

- In the **top bar**, tap the screen and type the web address – **URL** – you want to visit, using the on-screen keyboard. As you type, you'll see suggestions of previous pages you've visited, which you can **select** by tapping the address in the list. Tap **Go** when you've finished.

## Hot Tip

Made a mistake? Clear the address bar at any time by tapping the X button on the far right.

**Above:** To visit a website use the onscreen keyboard to type the web address and press go.

## Tab That

Just like your desktop browser, you can have several web pages open at once, in separate tabbed windows. To open a new window, tap the + button at the end of the tab bar and enter the web address. Switch between the windows by tapping the tab you want. To close just that page, tap the X button in the left corner.

## Cloud Button

If you've been surfing the web using Safari on your Mac, you can carry on from the same place on your iPad by tapping the Cloud icon in the Safari toolbar. This will show you the tabs that are currently open on your other iOS devices and Mac (if it's running the latest operating system, Mountain Lion), provided they are also set up to use iCloud.

# FASTER BROWSING

iPad 3, 4 and mini support the new 4G technology, which enables much faster browsing and quicker download speeds for videos and such like.

## 4G LTE

The latest iPads with mobile connections support the next generation of mobile broadband – 4G LTE (Long Term Evolution). In fact, it's so 'next generation' that these 4G fourth generation networks aren't universally available yet and are still being rolled out in different countries. The advantage of 4G is that it

**Above:** Tap the cloud icon to access sites which are currently open on your Mac or other iOS devices which have iCloud activated.

is about five times faster than 3G and more reliable. Not only are browsing and downloading faster, but there's also less choppiness when you stream a video or watch TV – that is, fewer stops as the iPad struggles to keep up. Even without 4G, the new iPads support the latest and fastest versions of 3G. With their powerful new antennae inside they are less likely to lose the connection.

# NAVIGATING THE WEB

Just like your computer browser, Safari lets you move backwards and forwards between open web pages using the left and right pointers on the top bar. However, there are other novel ways to navigate individual pages.

## Viewing Web Pages

- **Scroll the page**: Drag your finger up and down the screen. The scrollbar on the right shows where you are. For faster scrolling, flick your finger up or down the page.

- **Unpinch**: This lets you zoom in on part of the page. Put two fingers together on the screen where you want to enlarge the page and move them apart. Put two fingers either side of the screen and move them together (pinch) to reverse this.

- **Zoom in to images** and text by double-tapping the screen. Zoom out by repeating the double-tap.

- **Once zoomed in**, tap the screen and drag the page left or right. A horizontal scrollbar at the bottom of the screen shows where you are on the page.

## Uncluttered Websites

Some web pages are so full of text and ads that they can be very difficult to read. Safari Reader solves this by presenting a stripped down version of the page. Tap the Reader button, to the right of the address field, and ads are removed, leaving just text and pictures. For extra readability, the text is shown against a shaded background and you can increase its size.

**Above:** You can navigate web pages by pinching and unpinching to zoom in and out, and dragging up and down to scroll.

## Private Browsing

If you don't want to leave a trail of the websites you've visited – such as the jewellery store where you have been looking for presents – turn on private browsing.

1. Go to Settings, Safari and switch on Private Browsing. Now Safari won't keep a list of sites you visit, although you also lose the convenience of Safari saving any website login details.

2. With Safari in private mode the top and bottom bars are black rather than the usual grey.

3. For further privacy you can also clear your history (the list of sites you have visited), as well as cookies and other website data.

## Watching Flash Videos

When browsing the web with Safari, you may find that videos on the page won't play, as they need Adobe Flash to run, which isn't supported on the iPad. Some sites, such as YouTube, get round this by automatically changing the video format in the background. If not, there are alternative browsers for the iPad that can play Flash, such as Skyfire, available from the App Store.

> **Hot Tip**
> The Reader button doesn't appear with every web page you view. It has to be supported by the website you're visiting, which many commercial sites won't do, as they want their ads to show.

**Above:** Select the Safari Reader button to display an uncluttered version of the webpage which has ads removed, leaving only text and pictures.

# SEARCH

Search the web, using your preferred search engine, direct from the iPad.

1. **The Search box**: This is on the right of Safari's top bar. Tap the box and use the pop-up keyboard to enter what you are searching for.

2. **As you type**: A list of suggestions will appear as you type. If none are correct, finish entering your text and tap the Search button on the keyboard.

3. **Search term**: You can also look for your search term on the web page you're currently viewing. Scroll to the end of the list of suggestions and tap On This Page.

4. **Google**: This the default search engine used by Safari. To change this, tap Settings, Safari, then Search Engine and select one you prefer.

# SAVE THE WEB

As you browse the web, Safari offers several ways to share the pages you like or save them for viewing later.

## Sharing

Tap the Share button on the top bar for various ways to spread the word about a web page. Mail the link, text it or post it to your status on Facebook and Twitter. For easy

**Above:** Press the Home button to search the web by dictating your request to Siri.

access, add it to your Home Screen or Reading List and you can always bookmark or print it, if an AirPrint printer is available.

## Reading List

If you don't have time to read something that interests you, view it later. Tap the Share button, then touch Add to Reading List. The page isn't stored on your iPad but is synced with iCloud, so you can access the page, using any of your iOS devices, via the internet.

## Hot Tip

Instead of repeatedly filling in your personal contact details on web forms, use AutoFill. Enable it by tapping Settings, Safari and selecting AutoFill preferences.

To view your Reading List, tap Bookmarks and then press the link. Once you have visited the page, it no longer shows in the Unread list but can still be accessed by the All tab.

# BOOKMARKS

To add a page to your bookmarks, tap the Share button, then Bookmark. To access your bookmarks, tap the open book icon on the top bar. Using iCloud, you can synchronize your bookmarks between your iPad, computer and other iOS devices, so you always have access to your favourite web pages.

To change your bookmarks, tap Edit in the top corner. Press the red '–' sign to delete one. To reorder your bookmarks, tap and hold the three-line grab handles and move them up or down the list. When finished, tap Done.

**Left** View, visit and reorder your bookmarked pages by tapping the open book icon in the top bar.

# MESSAGING

**Need to send a message to a friend? Using the built-in Messages app, you can text anyone who has an iPhone, iPod Touch or iPad for free – and even send pictures or video.**

**Step 1:** Check iMessage is turned on by selecting the Messages option within Settings.

**Step 4:** Tap the New Message icon, start typing in the To box to bring up other iMessage users.

## TEXTING

The beauty of iMessage, the name that Apple has given to its messaging system, is that since iOS 5 it is built in.

### How to Text: Step-by-step

1.  Go to Settings, Messages and make sure that iMessage is turned on.

2.  Launch the Messages app. If it's not already entered, you'll have to give your Apple ID and password to activate the service. Tap Sign In.

3.  Enter the email address you want use to send messages. It can be any you own; it doesn't have to be the same one used with your Apple ID. Tap Next.

4.  Open Messages and tap the new message icon (pen and paper) at the top of the screen. Start writing in the To: line and a pop-up box listing your relevant contacts will appear. You can send a message to any name that has a blue speech bubble beside it.

5. Tap the name of the selected iMessage user, type your message and press the blue Send button.

6. In true messaging style, your conversation is shown as a series of speech bubbles: your message on the right, your friend's reply on the left. When someone is replying to you, there's a bubble with three dots in the chat window.

## Group Messaging

You can send messages to a group. For example, to let everyone know what the arrangements are for an evening out, just write their names in the To: line or select them from your Contacts using the + button.

## Go Multimedia

To add a picture tap the Camera icon beside the text box. In the pop-up box, choose to send an existing image from your photo library or select Take Photo or Video (if you have one of the later iPads with a camera) and add a new picture or video clip.

## Person Icon

Tap on the Person icon and you have all the contact details of the person you are in conversation with. Click the Edit button to change them (not iPad 1).

## Cleaning Up

Tap the forward button in the chat window and you can select individual parts of the conversation to email on – or delete (not iPad 1). To remove the whole conversation swipe your finger from right to left and tap the Delete button.

**Step 5**: After selecting the recipient, type your message and press the send button.

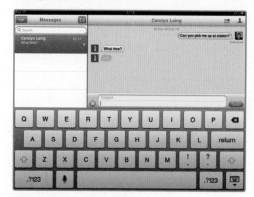

**Step 6**: Sent and received messages are shown in speech bubbles.

# EMAIL

If you can't bear to be parted from your email, the Mail app lets you connect to your online mailbox and will even notify you when you've got mail.

## SETTING UP ACCOUNTS

To access your email, you first need to set up details of your email service. With some of the main email programs, such as Microsoft Outlook or Apple Mail, you can transfer these settings using iTunes. Otherwise, you can do it directly on your iPad.

### Transfer Your Email Settings

1.  First, connect your iPad with your computer, using a USB cable or wirelessly over your Wi-Fi network.

2.  Open iTunes on your computer and you'll see your iPad listed on the top bar.

3.  Click on the Info tab and go to Sync Mail Accounts. Select the accounts you want on your iPad and click Apply or Sync. Only your account settings – none of your emails – are copied across.

### Add Email Accounts Direct to Your iPad

Although you access your emails through the Mail app, you set up the account using the main Settings app.

1.  Tap Settings, then Mail, Contacts, Calendars and Add Account.

2.  You will see several of the most popular web-based mail services  listed, including Gmail, Microsoft Hotmail, AOL, Yahoo! and Apple's iCloud. There's also Microsoft Exchange,

which is used by many schools and companies for their email servers.

3. Tap the button for your email service if it's listed and enter your name, email address, password and a description, then tap Save.

4. If it's not listed, select Other and enter your account details manually – you can get them from your Internet Service Provider.

**Step 2**: Choose your email provider from the list, or tap Other to add your account details.

# CONFIGURING MAIL

There are several ways to customize Mail and keep up-to-date with your emails without being overwhelmed.

## Preferences

Select how you want to organize your emails in Settings, Mail, Contacts, Calendars, then scroll to Mail.

- **Show**: This selects how many messages, from 50 to 1,000, to display in your inbox.

- **Preview**: Change how many lines of text from each email are shown in List view.

- **Show To/Cc Label**: This shows if you are the main recipient of an email or if it was copied to you.

- **Ask Before Deleting**: This is a useful precaution if you often delete emails accidentally.

○ **Load Remote Images**: Turn this off to save bandwidth, if you often download your email over a mobile connection.

○ **Organize By Thread**: Turn this on and all replies to an email will be grouped under the original message.

Other options let you send a blind copy of every outgoing email to yourself; indent text quoted in a reply; and set the default email account to be used by iPad apps.

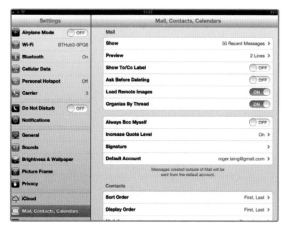

**Above**: Choose how your emails are organized by toggling options On or Off in the Mail settings list.

## Configuring How Email Is Received

Where it's supported, you can have new emails pushed to you automatically or fetched from the server at a set interval you determine.

1.  Tap Settings, then Mail, Contacts, Calendars and select Fetch New Data.

**Above**: Choose whether to receive your emails by Push or Fetch, and how frequently this will happen.

2.  If you have an email service where the server will automatically 'push' any new emails received to you, such as iCloud or Microsoft Exchange, then select Push.

3. If not, select Fetch. Then choose how frequently you want Mail to check for new emails, ranging from Every 15 Minutes to Hourly. The more frequently it checks, the greater the drain on your battery.

4. Tap Advanced, select each account and then choose which schedule you want to apply. Selecting Manual effectively turns off automatic email checking.

## Hot Tip

**Signature adds your personal sign off to every email you send. Go to Settings, Mail, Contacts, Calendars, then choose Signature and enter your text. This is also where you delete the annoying default signature added by Apple: *Sent from my iPad*.**

# WORKING WITH EMAIL

Use the built-in Mail app to send and receive your emails when you are connected to the internet.

## Using Mail

Mail shows all your inboxes – the mailboxes for incoming emails – in one list with the Accounts underneath.

- At the top of the list is **All Inboxes**. This is a **single inbox** for all the emails you receive from any account. Alternatively, you can select the inbox for an **individual account**, such as your main personal or work account.

- The list appears **automatically** when the iPad is in **landscape view**. In **portrait view** flick your finger from the **left** of the screen to show the list; flick from the **right** side of the screen to close it again.

## Receive Mail

1. When you tap the inbox, there's a list of all your emails. Each one shows the sender's name, when it was sent, the subject line and a preview of the first few lines of the message.

2.  Drag the list down to check for new messages. Tap the message preview, and the full message opens in the main window.

3.  If you tap the sender's name, you have the option to add them as a new contact or add the email address to an existing contact. You can also add them to your VIP list.

4.  A numbered grey icon on the right shows how many messages are grouped together into a thread, because they all have the same subject line.

5.  Flick to scroll through the message or messages if it's a thread. Double-tap or pinch to zoom in on the text or images. Touch and hold an image for options to save, copy or share it.

6.  If there's a word in the message you're not familiar with, look it up. Double-tap to select the word, using the grab handles if necessary, and then tap Define in the pop-up menu bar.

7.  To zip back to the start of the email, tap the iPad status bar at the top of the screen.

**Above:** Tapping the name of an email sender gives you the option to add the address to your contact or VIP lists.

## Organize Your Messages

Along Mail's top bar are several icons that help you organize your messages.

○  **Flag:** Tap this and select Flag to show the message is important (it will appear with an Orange flag beside it in the list)

### Hot Tip

Tap and hold the Home button and ask Siri to 'check my email', and a list of the latest emails appears. Tap the one you want, and it opens in the main Mail window. (iPad 3, 4 and mini only.)

or Mark as Unread (which is shown by a small blue circle).

- **Folder**: Tap, and the list box shows the folders (mailboxes) for that account. Select a folder, and the message is moved there.

- **Bin**: This deletes the message.

- **Arrow**: Tap this for options to Reply, Forward or Print your message.

- **Edit**: Use this to apply an action to several messages at once. Tap the Edit button at the top of the Inboxes List, then touch the messages you want. Press the Delete, Move or Mark (as Unread) buttons as required.

**Above**: Tap the flag icon in Mail's top bar to Flag an important message or Mark as Unread.

**Above**: To find particular emails stored in your mail box, type a phrase in the search box and select the relevant option to choose where to search.

## Search

This is handy if you want to find that elusive email or group together several on the same topic or from the same person. Tap in the Search box and enter your phrase. Then tap the relevant button for where to search – the From or To fields, the Subject line or the new ALL option, which searches the body of the message as well. From the results, select the emails you want and click the Edit button to delete/archive, move or mark them, as appropriate.

## Delete Messages

To delete a message, flick its title in the message list. If the email is open, you can also use the delete button in the top bar. To delete several emails at once, click the Edit button, select the messages and click the red delete button.

## Deleting the Archive

Given the huge amounts of space some services offer for email storage, some email providers, such as Gmail, don't delete messages but archive them.

1.  Flick across a message in the list and the normal Delete button is shown as Archive. Tap this and the message is removed from that inbox but still remains in the All Mail folder.

2.  To properly delete the message and send it to the Bin instead of the Archive, tap Settings, then Mail, Contacts, Calendars. Tap the relevant account and turn off Archive Messages.

### Hot Tip

If you forward an email, you can include attachments from the original, which you can't if you just Reply to a message.

**Above:** Forward a message by clicking on the curved arrow at the top of an email and select the Forward option.

## Send Email: Step-by-step

1.  To write a new email, tap the Paper and Pen icon at the top of Mail or if you're replying or forwarding a message, select the curved arrow at the top.

2.  In the New Message box that opens, add the recipient's email address. You can type this in or tap the + sign to select them from your Contacts list.

3.  If you choose the wrong name, simply tap it and press the backspace key on the keyboard to delete it.

4.  Add anyone you're copying the message to. Use Bcc – blind copying – if you're sending it to lots of people, such as a mailing list, and you don't want to show all their addresses.

5.  Tap From and choose the account you are using to send it. Add your Subject line and type your message.

6.  To format the text, tap and use the grab handles to select all the text you want to include. Tap BIU and then choose Bold, Italic or Underline. From this menu you can also choose Quote Level to increase or decrease the indentation on any text quoted from the original message.

**Hot Tip**

You can resize photo attachments, which is particularly useful when sending your email over a mobile connection. Once the photo is attached, tap Image size in the header section and choose Small, Medium or Large, as appropriate.

7.  To add an attachment, tap where you want to add it and select Insert Photo or Video from the pop-up menu. Select the photo source, then the photo and tap the Use button.

8.  When you're happy with your message, press the Send button in the top-right corner. If you're not yet ready to send, tap the Cancel button and choose the Save Draft option.

# VIP MAIL

This is a new feature in iOS 6 (not available on iPad 1). Messages from people you choose as important to you – your family, best friend, boss, etc. – appear in their own VIP mailbox. They also have a VIP star icon beside them in the message preview.

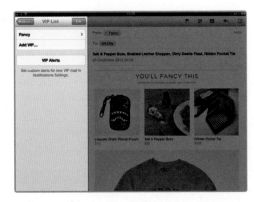

## Adding VIPs

○  **To add a sender to your VIP list**: Tap their name in the From field in an email and select Add to VIP from the pop-up box.

○  **To manage your VIP list**: Touch the white arrow in a blue circle icon. Here you can add more people and set up alerts for the arrival of VIP mail.

**Above:** Tap the white arrow in a blue circle to add and remove contacts to your VIP list and set up alerts.

# VIDEO CALLING

**If you have an iPad 2 or later, you can use the built-in cameras to have great video chats with other Apple users via FaceTime or use Skype to reach more of your contacts.**

**Above:** Activate FaceTime by selecting the FaceTime option in your settings list and toggling to On.

## FACETIME

With the iPad's FaceTime app you can make free video calls over the internet anywhere in the world.

### Setting up Your Video Calls

As well as a camera-equipped iPad, you'll need to be connected to the internet to use FaceTime. The person you are calling must also have an iPad, iPhone or iPod Touch with forward-facing camera or a Mac computer with camera and FaceTime.

1.  Before you start, activate FaceTime by going to Settings, then FaceTime.

2.  FaceTime identifies you through your Apple ID, the email address and password you use for accessing the App Store. You can either use your existing ID or create a new one.

3.  Next, select which of your email addresses to use as your contact point with your FaceTime account.

4.  With the latest release of the iPad operating system, iOS 6, you can use your mobile connection for video chat. However, depending on your price plan, a FaceTime chat could use up much of your monthly data allowance and with 3G connections the quality may be

poor. Turn off Use Cellular Data and FaceTime will work only on Wi-Fi.

## FaceTime Calls: Step-by-Step

1. To make a FaceTime call, tap the FaceTime app to open it. A list of your contacts is on the right. If the person you want isn't listed, tap the + icon, add their details and tap Done.

2. To make a call, tap the name of the person, then their FaceTime phone number or email address.

3. When they answer, there will be a pause while the video chat is set up. Once connected, your face will shrink to a small thumbnail, while the person you are calling is pictured in the main window.

4. During the call, drag your picture to a different position if it's in the way.

5. Tap the microphone icon on the menu to temporarily mute sound (the picture won't be affected). Tap again to restore it.

6. Tap the camera icon to switch from the front camera, showing you, to the back camera, which will show what's around you.

7. To finish the chat, tap the telephone icon marked End.

**Step 3**: Video images of yourself and your contact appear once the call is set up.

**Step 5**: Tap the microphone icon to mute sound, and tap again to unmute.

**Step 6**: Tap the camera icon to change between using your front and back iPad cameras.

## Hot Tip

You can switch apps during a chat, if, for example, you want to look something up. Press the Home button, then the icon for the app you want. You can still chat but there will be no picture. Tap the green bar at the top of the screen to resume the video call.

## SKYPE

Unlike FaceTime, Skype offers free video and voice chat that lets you stay in touch with friends and family no matter what computer or mobile device they use. Owned by Microsoft, it also replaces their highly popular instant messaging program, Windows Live Messenger.

## Using Skype: Step-by-step

Before using Skype, you have to set up an account. Open your Safari web browser on the iPad and type in the address www.skype.com.

1. On the Home page tap the blue Join Skype button and fill in the form, which includes creating your Skype username and password. Alternatively, you can sign up using a Microsoft account, such as Messenger or Hotmail, an email programme like Outlook or your Facebook account.

2. If you haven't already, download the Skype for iPad app from iTunes. Open the app and enter your Skype sign in details.

3. Skype asks permission to add your contacts. Alternatively, you can tap the + button in the top-right corner and choose Search Skype Directory to look for people you know.

Step 3: Tap the + button in the top right corner to search the Skype Directory for people you want to add to your contact list.

4. Once you have discovered them, select them and in the screen that opens tap Add Contact. Enter a message asking them to accept you as a contact and tap send.

5.  Once you have built up your Contacts list, simply tap the contact you want to call. Choose the type of call you want to make – it can be a Video Call, Voice Call or Chat (Instant Messaging conversation).

6.  The controls are much the same as for FaceTime, with the menu bar at the bottom and the main window displaying the video with your picture inset.

7.  To send a text message during your video chat, tap the message icon – a blue speech bubble – and type it in the pop-up box that appears. Tap the message button again to close the window.

8.  End the call by tapping the phone receiver icon.

9.  By default, Skype will always show you as online, even when the app is only running in the background. You can change this by going to Settings, then Skype and tapping Go Offline. Here you can choose to go offline immediately you quit Skype or after a suitable interval ranging from 15 to 60 minutes.

## Phone Home, Cheaply

As Skype-to-Skype voice calls are free, they are a very popular way for people to stay in touch, wherever they are in the world, without running up huge phone bills. Low-cost calls can also be made to ordinary landline phones and mobiles by signing up to Skype's unlimited plan or buying pay-as-you-go credit.

**Hot Tip**

You can chat with anyone, anywhere using the Skype app with a Wi-Fi or 3G connection on any iPad. But while you can send and receive video using the front or back camera with the iPad 2 or above, you can only receive video on the first generation iPad.

**Above:** If you do not want to always appear 'Online', change your Skype settings to 'Go Offline'.

# SOCIAL MEDIA

**The popularity of social media is such that Apple has built support for Facebook and Twitter in to the iPad operating system itself. Now you can Tweet, update your status, post a photo, your location or a link direct from several of the built-in apps.**

## FACEBOOK

As one of the most popular sites on the web, with more than one billion users, it's natural that Facebook is now directly accessible from your iPad.

### Setting up Facebook

Support for Facebook is built in to iOS 6. As a result you can do all you normally would, from browsing your wall to adding photos, without opening the Facebook app.

1.  To set up Facebook, tap Settings and then Facebook. If you haven't already installed the app, do so by clicking the Install button.

2.  Enter your Facebook Username and Password and tap Sign In. The pop-up window explains what you allow by signing into Facebook from the iPad's operating system. In essence, this is agreeing to:

    ○ **Merge** your Facebook friends' details with your Contacts, so that if they update their details, their entry in your Contacts is also immediately updated.

**Above:** If your iPad can run iOS 6, set up Facebook through your Settings for an integrated social networking experience.

○ **Download** your Facebook events to your calendar.

○ **Allow** you to post photos, update your status, and send messages and other content to Facebook.

○ **Enable** other apps on your iPad to access your Facebook account. To do so, they first have to ask your permission and make clear what information they will use and how. You can withdraw your permission at any time.

3. If you don't accept this, tap the Cancel button; otherwise touch Sign In.

4. Ironically, having just allowed Facebook to access your Contacts and Calendar, you can now refuse either one or both, by turning off the button beside the relevant icon in the Allow These Apps to Use Your Account section.

5. If you tap Update All Contacts, your information will be shared with Facebook, so they can update photos and usernames.

## Hot Tip

On the original iPad you can upgrade the operating system to iOS 5, which includes Twitter integration. But unlike later iPads it can't run iOS 6, which also introduced Facebook integration. The only way to access Facebook on iPad 1 is to download the standalone app from iTunes.

**Above:** Choose whether you want Facebook to have access to your Contacts and Calendar by toggling the buttons to On or Off.

## Using Facebook on the iPad

○ **Update your status**: Pull down the Notification Tray from the top of any screen and tap the Facebook icon to open the Status Update box. Write your message, then tap the Post button.

○ **Share URLs:** When you're browsing the internet with Safari and come across a link you'd like to post on Facebook, tap the Share button, then Facebook.

○ **Send pictures:** To send photos direct from your photo library or camera, select the image you want to post in Photos, tap the Share button and then Facebook. In the Update box you'll see the image with the name of the photo album on Facebook to which it will be posted. In Camera, tap the roll of images, then press the Share button and Facebook as above.

○ **Share your current location:** In the Maps app, tap the pin that marks where you are, then the blue arrow. Tap Share Location and select Facebook.

○ **Like apps, music and more:** The Facebook Like button is now in iTunes and the App Store, so you can show your friends what you appreciate without leaving the page. To add a comment, tap the Share button at the top-right of the Description page and select Facebook.

○ **Location:** In the Facebook Status Update box add your location by tapping the arrow in the bottom-left corner. Choose who you want to share it with by tapping the Friends icon and selecting from the list.

**Above:** Share your location over Facebook by tapping your location in the Maps app and choosing the Share Location option, and then selecting Facebook.

## Ask Siri to Update Your Friends

Siri can also update your Facebook status for you. Hold the Home button to launch Siri, say 'Post to Facebook' and dictate your message. Anything said after Facebook will be posted to your wall. (iPad 3, 4 and mini only.)

# Hot Tip

**For easy Facebook posting,
the Share Widget must be enabled.
Go to Notifications, select
Share Widget and turn on
Notification Centre.**

# TWITTER

The social networking and micro-blogging site, where every post is 140 characters or fewer, was the first to be fully integrated with the iPad. You can send a Tweet and add pictures or your location, without using the Twitter app.

## Setting up Twitter

This is very similar to setting up Facebook. Go to Settings, Twitter. You can download and install the Twitter app, if you haven't already, although you can Tweet without it.

What you will need is a Twitter account. If you have one already, enter your details. If not, set one up here by tapping Create New Account. If, like many people, you have several accounts – one for your personal Tweets, another for a business or a hobby – then tap Add Account and enter the details. Now you are already signed in and ready to go, whether or not you use the standalone Twitter app.

## Tweeting: Step-by-step

1. Simply pull down the Notification Tray from the top of any screen and click the Tap to Tweet box. Your Twitter username is already entered in the message box.

2. To send from a different account, if you have one, tap your username and select the one you want from the list.

**Step 1:** When Tweeting from the Notifications tray, change between accounts by tapping the username box and selecting the relevant name from the drop down list.

3. As you enter your message, the number at the bottom-right shows how many of the available 140 characters remain. When finished, tap Send.

4. You can also ask Siri to 'Send a Tweet'. Siri will open a Tweet box and ask: 'OK, what \would you like your message to say?' Dictate your message, and when it's correct, say 'Send' (only available on iPad 3 and later).

## Tweeting Photos and Your Location: Step-by-step

If you have a photo you must share with your Twitter followers, it's easy to do through your iPad.

1. In either Photos or the Camera app (if you have an iPad2 or later), select the image and tap the Share button, then Twitter.This opens the Tweet box, with the photo clipped to the side. As before, choose the account to send it from and add your message. Notice that the image (in fact it's the shortened URL of where the image is stored) takes up a number of characters and reduces the amount left for your message.

2. To add your location, tap the arrow and tap Enable to allow Twitter to share your location. The arrow turns purple once you're located. If you decide you don't want to share your location after all, tap the X.

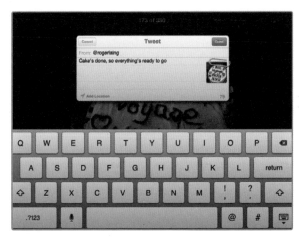

3. Alternatively, simply Tweet your location from within Maps. Tap the pin marking your location, then the blue i button and select Share Location, then Twitter.

**Step 1:** Tweet a photo by selecting an image from your Photos or Camera Roll, tapping the Share button, and choosing the Twitter option.

4. The message My Current Location is automatically added to the Tweet box. Delete this and add your own if you prefer. Again the character count is reduced because of the attached location information. Tap Send to post to Twitter.

## Hot Tip

To be notified when you receive a direct message or mention in Twitter, tap Settings, Notifications, Twitter and slide the switch for Notification Centre to On.

## Merge Contacts with Twitter

With Twitter built in to the system, you can merge your friends' Twitter usernames or avatars and pictures with your Contacts. Go to Settings, Twitter and tap the Update Contacts button. Now if you tap on a contact's Twitter name you have the option to send them a Tweet or see all their recent Tweets – without having to visit Twitter.

## Using the Apps

There are many different apps on the iPad, from Tweetbot or Friendly to the Twitter and Facebook apps themselves, which offer a similar rich experience to the one you get online: you can send direct messages, find followers, see who's following you, add friends and so on. What the integration with iOS offers is convenience – now, when you come across something you want to share, you can do so with a couple of taps regardless of which app you're using.

**Above:** Apps such as Tweetbot can be downloaded from the App Store if you want a more comprehensive Twitter experience which involves viewing trending hashtags, browsing your Twitter Feed, seeing who is following you, and sending direct messages.

# LOCATION SERVICES

**Whether it's forecasting the weather where you are or finding the nearest pizza restaurant, more and more apps are using the iPad's Location Services.**

## FIND YOURSELF

Location Services combine information from the iPad's built-in compass with Wi-Fi, mobile and GPS data to locate where you are.

### Find My Friends: Step-by-step

Although the idea of tracking people is a little sinister, no one can be tracked without giving their permission.

1.  Go to the App Store and download the free Find My Friends app (which installs as Find Friends).

**Above:** Enter your contacts' names or email addresses to request them to share their location with you using the Find My Friends app. You will then be able to view their location on the map.

2.  Log in to the service using your Apple ID. Allow the app to Use your Current Location, and the compass arrow appears in the top bar.

3.  Now ask your friends to share their location. Tap the Add Friends button, type in their email address or contact name, if you allowed the app to access your Contacts, add your message and tap Send.

4.  When your friend accepts, you can see their location but they can't see yours. To do so, they have to ask your permission. If they do, you'll see it under Requests.

5.  Once you are following a number of friends, you can see their location on the map, each one marked with a purple dot. Your location is marked by a blue dot.

## Temporary Sharing

This is great if you and your friends are planning to meet up for an evening. They can track you to make sure they go to the right location.

1.  Tap Temporary then the + icon. Add the people you're inviting, give the event a name and tap beside Ends to set a date and time when the location sharing ends. This can be a few hours or several days.

2.  Tap Me at the bottom and you can see your current location, and add a label for easy reference. In the box on the left you also have a list of who's following you.

# EXPLORE WITH MAPS

The iPad now has its own Maps app, which enables you to go local – and find the nearest French restaurant or cinema complex – or international. It provides step-by-step directions and also shows traffic conditions.

## Getting Started with Maps

An internet connection – either Wi-Fi or mobile – is needed for Maps to draw down the mapping information. It also relies on Location Services for many of its features. Make sure these are on by going to Settings, Privacy, and turning on Location Services and then Maps.

> **Hot Tip**
>
> On iPads with Wi-Fi and Cellular (3G and 4G), the built-in GPS will be used to determine your location more accurately, which can run down your battery faster.

**Above:** Activate Maps by making sure it is toggled to On in the Settings menu.

## Redrawing the World

Apple Maps was introduced with iOS 6 and has had a few teething problems, most notably misplacing several major cities. Apple has promised to improve the app but isn't likely to return to the previous version, based on Google maps, although that is still available on the original iPad.

## Find a Location

1. Tap the Maps app, then type the name of the place you're looking for in the Search bar. You can search by geographic features, place names, neighbourhood names, street addresses, landmarks, business names and so on. Maps also takes your location into account, so will look for King Street, London in the UK, if you're there, before looking in Australia or elsewhere.

2. If you're looking for somewhere nearby, such as a coffee shop or theatre, tap the compass arrow to zoom in on your current location.

3. Maps drops several pushpins on the map with a black bar over the best match. Tap the i icon to open the Info window.

4. This tells you more about the location and may include photos, reviews, directions to and from the location, or a link to the website. It also has options to add it to Contacts, share the location on Facebook and Twitter or bookmark it.

## Change the View

Tap or drag the page curl at the bottom-right corner of the screen and you can change the way you look at the location.

**Above**: Tap the i icon to open the Info window to find out more information about the location the pin is marking, including photos, reviews and directions. You can also share the location with others.

- **Standard**: This is the normal map-style.

- **Hybrid**: This has place and street names on top of the satellite photos.

- **Satellite**: Thi sas overhead photographic views.

- **3D**: Tap the 3D button in the bottom-left or drag two fingers up from the bottom of the screen to zoom in on the map and tilt it. If HD resolution satellite pictures are available for the location, the 3D button changes to a Flyover button.

## Get Directions

To get directions to a location, by car, on foot or using public transport, tap the Directions button. Enter where you are and where you're going in the Start and End fields. Maps displays the route – and any alternatives – along with time and distance information.

## Check Traffic En Route

Tap the paper curl in the bottom-right and then Show Traffic to see what road conditions are like (where the service is available). Orange dots mark slow moving traffic, red dots show stop-go driving, while other icons warn of roadworks and accidents.

## Step-by-step Navigation

With the help of Siri, Maps offers step-by-step GPS navigation, similar to the sat-nav in a car or handheld system. It will also store maps of a very large surrounding area so you can still browse and use GPS navigation when you are outside Wi-Fi or mobile data coverage.

**Above:** Maps will display alternative routes to your destination, with times and distances noted.

## Hot Tip

Let Siri be your travelling companion. Siri can find locations, tell you what points of interest or services are nearby and get directions for your trip (iPad 3 and above).

PHOTOGRAPHS & VIDEO

# YOUR PHOTOS

**The iPad is the complete photographer's kit – able to capture great photos, display them in their full beauty on a high-definition screen and store thousands of pictures in your own electronic album.**

## TAKE AMAZING PHOTOS

As a hand-held camera, the iPad is bulky but with both a front and backward-facing lens, it can provide consistently good results.

### Camera App

Cameras were first introduced with the iPad 2 and have been significantly upgraded since.

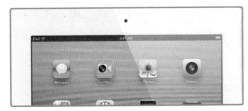

**Above:** The iPad's front camera is very useful for Facetime.

**Above:** The rear camera allows you to view shots on screen first.

|  | iPad 1 | iPad 2 | iPad 3 | iPad 4 | iPad mini |
|---|---|---|---|---|---|
| Front camera | None | FaceTime Camera | FaceTime HD Camera | FaceTime HD Camera | FaceTime HD Camera |
| Photos |  | 0.3 Megapixel VGA- resolution | 0.3 Megapixel VGA- resolution | 1.2 Megapixel | 1.2 Megapixel |
| Video |  | 0.3 Megapixel VGA- resolution | 0.3 Megapixel VGA- resolution | 720p HD video | 720p HD video |
| FaceTime Video |  | Wi-Fi | Wi-Fi + Cellular | Wi-Fi + Cellular | Wi-Fi + Cellular |
| Rear camera | None | Back camera | iSight |  |  |
| Photos |  | 0.7 Megapixel | 5 Megapixel | 5 Megapixel | 5 Megapixel |
| Video |  | 720p HD video | 1080 HD video | 1080 HD video | 1080 HD video |

## Taking a Picture: Step-by-step

**1.** To take a picture, tap the Camera app. The animation of a shutter opens and you should see the image. If you're in the picture, you're using the forward-pointing camera.

**2.** To switch to the rear camera, tap the camera icon with the curved arrows either side. Make sure that the lower-right switch is set to camera and not video.

**3.** You'll see a square white box appear on the screen. This is the focus box. Tap anywhere on the image and the camera centres on that part of the picture.

**4.** When using the rear camera, tap the image with two fingers together and push them apart to zoom in on the area you want to shoot. A slider appears on the screen for more accurate control.

**5.** To help you frame your shot, you can also overlay a grid of thin white lines. Tap Options, slide the Grid switch to On and tap Done.

**Step 3**: Tap anywhere on screen to focus on that part of the picture, as indicated by a white frame.

**6.** When ready, take your shot by pressing the round camera icon on the screen. Alternatively, you can use the up and down volume button on the side of the iPad.

**7.** The pictures you've taken can be viewed in the Camera Roll, the small square box in the bottom-left corner. Tap the image to bring up the controls, which are the same as those in the Photos app. These let you view, share and edit your images. Tap Done to return to the camera.

# EDIT YOUR PHOTOS

However good or bad a photographer you are, the iPad's image-editing tools can make your pictures look better.

## Photos App

It's all too easy, in the rush to capture a moment, to end up with a less than perfect photo. The Photos app (for iPad 2 and later) gives you the basic tools to make your pictures better – whether they are images taken with the iPad itself, streamed through iCloud or uploaded from your digital camera.

**Hot Tip**

If you change your mind about the last edit tap the Undo button. If you want to undo all of the changes you've applied tap the Revert to Original button.

- **To start editing**: tap the Photos app with its easily recognizable sunflower icon.

- **To Edit**: Select the photo you want to enhance and tap the Edit button.

- **Editing tools**: Buttons for the four main editing tools appear at the bottom of the screen:

**Above:** Use the Photos app to edit your photos by rotating, enhancing, removing red-eye, cropping and constraining proportions.

1. **Rotate**: This lets you alter the angle of the picture to straighten the image.

2. **Enhance**: use the magic wand icon to adjust the colour and contrast of your images automatically.

3. **Red-eye**: Photos removes this by recolouring the eye. Tap the Red-Eye button and then on the mis-coloured eye. Tap on each eye affected, then press Apply to save your changes.

4. **Crop**: resize your pictures by tapping the Crop button and then pushing the corners of the grid that appears to adjust the frame. Reposition it to focus on the best bit of the photo. When finished, tap the Crop button in the top-right corner.

○ **Constrain**: If you're planning to print your photos, you can constrain the crop ratios to match. Simply press the Constrain button at the bottom and select the proportions you want.

# ADVANCED PHOTO EDITING

Make your pictures as eye-catching as possible, with iPad apps that offer the sort of sophisticated editing techniques usually found on more powerful computers.

## iPhoto App

Familiar to Mac computer users, iPhoto is also available as a paid-for app for the iPad 2 (and later). As well as editing your images and adding a variety of special effects, you can organize your photos and share them with friends and family.

○ **iPhoto**: Buy and install iPhoto from the App Store, then tap to open. It will import your library of images and display them as photo albums on a shelf.

○ **Albums**: One album will be your Camera Roll (photos taken with the iPad's cameras). Another is My Photo Stream, which will include any photos from other Apple devices, synced via iCloud.

○ **Tap Photos**: Do this, and you'll see thumbnail pictures of all the images on your iPad.

## Editing Photos with iPhoto

Select the photo you want to edit and tap the Edit button to bring up the photo-editing menu at the bottom of the screen.

**Hot Tip**
When you've used a tool to edit your photo, there is a blue marker above the button.

**Above:** Use the iPhoto editing screen to transform photos by altering properties and adding effects.

**Above:** The Brushes tool can be used to perfect an image in ways such as removing flaws.

○ **Crop and Straighten:** Does your photo look as though it has been taken on board a yacht in a gale? Level things up, using the Crop and Straighten button. Tap the button and slowly adjust the wheel at the bottom until the horizon is level.

○ **Exposure:** Change the lightness, brightness and contrast of your photo with one handy control.

○ **Auto-Enhance:** Use the magic wand button to bring out the true colours in your photo. As with the Photos app, it automatically chooses the best settings.

○ **Color:** The tools gathered here, under the icon of a painter's palette, control colour. The first boosts all colours in your image, with others that focus on sky colour, greenery, skin tones and white balance.

○ **Brushes:** These let you touch up small areas of the image. There is a Repair brush to remove marks, a red-eye remover and other tools to soften, sharpen or darken the picture.

○ **Effects:** Want to age your photo or make it more artistic? Tap this tool to select the filter you want to add – such as turning your colour photo black-and-white – then swipe your finger through the thumbnails to choose which option to apply.

## Applying Edits

With several of the tools, you tap and hold the area of the image where you want to apply the change, then slide your finger in the direction shown by the arrows to increase or decrease the effect.

## Hot Tip

For more information on the tools and details of how to use them, tap the question mark icon on the top bar.

### Other Photo-editing Apps

While Apple's iPhoto has the advantage of being available across all your iOS devices and Mac computers, there are other equally good, if not better, photo-editing apps available from third-party developers. Among them are Adobe Photoshop Touch (iPad 2 and later) and Snapseed, which is one of the few tools that can work with the more limited processing power available on the iPad 1.

# ORGANIZING YOUR PHOTOS

Arranging your images in photo albums makes it easier to find the images you want and show them off.

## Create Photo Albums: Step-by-step

You can use the built-in Photos app to set up your albums on iPad 2 and later.

1.  Tap to open, then select Albums and tap the + sign in the top-left corner. In the New Album box enter a name, then tap Save.

2.  The Photos view shows all the images on your iPad. Scroll through and select the images you want to add to that album. As you select each one, it is marked with a blue tick in the lower-right corner. When happy with your selection, tap the Done button to add the photos to the new album.

**Step 1:** Create a new album by selecting the + sign from the album screen and entering the name into the New Album box.

3. If you already have an album and want to add more images to it, tap the Photos tab for a view of all your images and then press the Edit button. Select the photos you want, as above, and tap the Add To... button.

4. Choose Add to Existing Album to do just that. Alternatively, tap Add to New Album and create another album.

## Organize by Date
Tap Events, and your imported photos are arranged in date-stamped folders, so you can see all the images taken at a particular time.

## Organize by Place
Tap Places, and the pins on the map mark where you took the photos (if they are tagged with GPS locations). Tap the pin and see the photos taken in that location.

# ADDING EFFECTS
From stretching and twisting your face to creating your own comic book images, there is a range of apps to add special effects to your photos.

## Fun with Photo Booth
This works with any camera-equipped iPad, using either the front or rear camera. Tap to open Photo Booth and choose the effect you want. Depending on the one you choose, you can pinch, swipe or rotate the image to alter the intensity of the effect.

**Hot Tip**
The Places button won't appear unless you are using Places in your Mac desktop version of iPhoto.

**Above:** Photo Booth allows you to alter an image in many different ways by choosing various effects.

1. Tap the camera to take the shot, which will be preceded by white flash. The picture appears in the photo roll at the bottom of the screen.

2. Tap the Share button and you can email, copy or delete it. It is automatically saved to the Camera Roll, from where you have more options to save and share it.

## Instagram

The photo-sharing app has been a massive hit with iPhone users since it launched. It lets you take a photo, choose a filter to change its look and feel, then post it to Instagram for friends and family to view. Surprisingly, though, given the iPad's superior screen, there's no native iPad app, so you have to use the iPhone version.

**Above:** There is no Instagram app for iPad, but you can download the iPhone version from the App Store.

### Add Text to Your Photos

Remember the Polaroid instant camera with the thick white border around the images that you could write on? Instant app recreates the Polaroid effect and even includes different handwriting fonts for adding your text.

### Comic Book Effect

Create your own comic strip with ComicBook! It turns you and your friends into stars of your own comic book in seconds, and you can publish direct to Facebook.

### Other Effects

There are iPad-specific apps to add virtually any effect you can think of – from vintage film-star looks to pop art – and then combine them in unusual ways to create collages, moodboards, posters and the like.

# VIEWING PHOTOS

**The iPad's display is great for showing off your photos, and if you have one with the Retina screen, they'll look even better.**

## PHOTO DISPLAYS

The iPad is a wonderfully portable digital photo album that can deliver slide shows or be an electronic picture frame.

### Album Photos

1. Open Photos, tap the Albums button, and you'll see various ones listed. These correspond to those you have in iPhoto or any picture folders you sync from your computer.

2. Tap on the album, and you'll see all the individual photos. Tap on any photo to view it up close. Tap the album name in the top-left to return to a view of all the photos.

3. Tap Albums at the top-left corner to return to the list of albums.

4. Alternatively, put a finger at the top and bottom of the screen and pinch them together to pull the photos back into album view.

### Hot Tip

**Retina is just Apple's marketing term to convey the extraordinary quality of screens with a high pixel density, where the average human retina can't make out individual pixels when seen from a normal viewing distance.**

**Step 2:** Tap on any individual photo in your album to view it close up.

## Slideshow

To make more of your photos, add music and fancy transition effects to create a slide show.

1.  In Photos, select the album or group of photos you want by tapping on the Photos, Events, Faces or Places button, then press the Slideshow button.

2.  Tap Transitions and select the effect you want to add between photos.

3.  To add your own soundtrack, turn on Play Music, then tap Music and select the song from your iTunes collection.

**Step 4:** Select slideshow options such as transitions and music and then tap the Start Slideshow button.

4.  Tap Start Slideshow to begin. To stop the slide show, tap anywhere on the screen.

## Picture Frame

When you're not working on your iPad, use it to display your photos.

1.  To set up your iPad as a digital picture frame, tap Settings, then Picture Frame. There's a choice of just two transitions – Dissolve or Origami.

2.  Select how long you want each photo to show for – from 2 to 20 seconds. Zoom in on Faces will show head-shots in close up.

3.  Turn on Shuffle to show your photos in a random order, then select the source of your images from those available in the Photos app.

## Hot Tip

If the picture frame is on public display, you might not want that photo of you asleep in a deck chair popping up. To avoid this, create your own photo album specifically for use with the Picture Frame.

4.  Turn your screen blank and lock your iPad by pressing the Wake/Sleep button at the top, then access the lock screen by pressing the Home button once.

5.  To the right of the slide to unlock box you'll see a button with a black-and-white flower icon. Tap this to start Picture Frame. Tap the screen again to get back to the lock screen and start using the iPad.

## Deleting Photos

However embarrassing a photo is, it may not be possible to delete it from the iPad. You can only delete photos you've taken on the iPad, that have been uploaded via the camera connection kit, saved from your email or a website using Safari, or are in your Photo Stream.

○ **To delete a single photo:** Tap the photo you want to delete, then the dustbin icon and press the red Delete Photo button. If the photo is in more than one album, the button changes to Delete Everywhere.

**Above:** Delete groups of photos by selecting the Edit button and then tapping photos to delete, they will be marked with a blue tick. Once you have finished selecting, tap the Delete button.

○ **To delete a group of photos:** Tap the Edit button followed by each photo you want to delete. Those selected are marked with a tick. Tap the Delete button, then confirm by pressing the Delete Selected Photos button.

○ **No delete option:** In some albums there is no delete option, as these photos are copies of images synced with your computer. To delete them, go to your computer and remove the photos from any albums that sync with the iPad.

# SHOW PHOTOS ON A BIGGER SCREEN

The iPad screen uses a special technology – In-Plane Switching (IPS) – for better viewing from different angles. However, for a bigger display, wirelessly transmit your photos to other screens, such as your TV.

## Mirror Your Pictures with AirPlay

To do this, you'll need a second generation Apple TV or later. Despite its name, it is not a TV but a receiver that connects to your TV with a high-definition cable. Special AirPlay wireless technology mirrors what's on your iPad to the receiver, which displays it on your TV.

- **To connect successfully** you need an iPad 2 or later, and both your Apple TV and iPad have to be on the same wireless network.

- **To show off your photos**, open Photos, tap Albums and then select the one you want to display. Tap on the photo and select the AirPlay icon (a square screen with an upward-pointing arrow at its base).

**Above:** Use AirPlay to show your photos on Apple TV by tapping on a selected photo and selecting the Airplay icon and then the Apple TV option.

- **Select Apple TV** and your photo will appear on the TV screen. You can flick between images, zoom in, pause and move from landscape to portrait view, and the changes will be reflected on the big screen.

## Physically Connect Your iPad Display and TV

An alternative way to mirror what's on your iPad screen to a TV or other display is through a physical connection. You'll need an Apple Digital AV adapter or VGA adapter. Plug this into your iPad and then connect it to an High Density Multimedia Interface (HDMI) cable from the TV or other display.

# ADDING PHOTOS

**There are numerous ways to put photos onto the iPad to take advantage of its high-quality display.**

## SAVED PHOTOS

Whether it's direct from the camera, if you have a camera-equipped iPad, or images from the web, you can save them all to the Photos app.

### Add Photos with the Camera

Photos taken with the cameras built in since iPad 2 appear automatically in the Camera Roll. Access this directly by tapping the square icon in the bottom-left of the Camera app.

### Add Photos from Other Apps

○ **Safari**: As you browse the web, you'll come across images you want to save, such as a picture of an ideal holiday destination. Tap and hold the image you want. In the box that opens, select Save Image and it will be downloaded to your Camera Roll.

○ **Messages**: Tap the image you've been sent and in the image box that opens click the Share button in the top-right corner and select Save to Camera Roll.

## Hot Tip

If you use Photo Booth to apply special effects to your photos, these will also appear in the Camera Roll album.

**Above**: To download a photo to your Camera Roll from Safari, tap and hold the image and then select the Save Image option.

◷ **Email**: Tap the email with the image attached then press the left-pointing arrow in the top bar. Select Save Image. It will show if there's more than one image attached and will save them all to the Camera Roll.

## Screenshots

Want to capture an image of what's on your iPad screen – such as your highest ever score on a favourite game? Press the Sleep/Wake button at the top of the iPad and the Home button at the same time then release. There'll be a flash of white light, a camera click and the image will appear in your Camera Roll. This is how the screenshots for this book were taken.

# UPLOADED PHOTOS

To transfer photos direct from your digital camera, you need a separate adapter. Alternatively, upload them first to your computer and use one of a growing number of third-party apps to transfer them wirelessly to the iPad.

### Camera Connection Kit

This kit, available from Apple, fits the iPad's original 30-pin dock connector design. It is the only way you can upload photos (and videos) direct from your camera. Each kit contains two adapters: one for the USB cable from your camera, the other for a Secure Digital (SD) memory card. Similar adapters for the Lightning connection on iPad 4 and mini are sold separately.

**Above:** Download photos directly from your digital camera using an SD memory card connection kit

### Importing Photos with the Adapters

Once you've made the physical connection, open Photos, if it hasn't already opened automatically.

1. Tap individual photos to select them, then press Import. To upload all the photos, tap Import All.

2.  You'll be asked if you want to delete the original photos from the camera or memory card once you've imported them.

3.  In Photos, tap Albums, Last Import to see the photos.

**Step 1:** Download the PhotoSync app to transfer photos to your iPad from other devices wirelessly.

### Wireless Transfer

There are several apps, such as PhotoSync, used here, which let you wirelessly transfer your photos to the iPad from either your computer or other iDevices. PhotoSync will sync your images with online photo storage sites, such as Flickr, Dropbox and Facebook. It can transfer from one to a thousand pictures at a time.

1.  Install the app on the iPad and any other iOS device you are using, as well as your Mac or PC.

2.  Go to Settings, Privacy, Location Services (just Location Services on iPad 1) and turn on for PhotoSync, so the app can access your photo library.

3.  Transfer your photos directly using the Wi-Fi network or Bluetooth, or via your web browser.

# SYNCED PHOTOS

To make sure you have all your latest photos on the iPad, sync your photos using iTunes or automatically download the most recent shots via iCloud.

### Photo Stream

This links up all your iOS devices or computers running iCloud so you can share any photos automatically. You just need to turn Photo Stream on.

1. Go to Settings, iCloud, Photo Stream and switch (My) Photo Stream on. Now if you take a photo on one device, like your iPad, it will appear in all others that have Photo Stream running.

2. Photo Stream stores the last 1,000 photos on iCloud, including those from the last 30 days. To view them on your iPad, tap Photos to open the app then the Photo Stream button.

3. Remember to move them from here to another album, share them or delete them before they are replaced as part of the normal rotation of photos.

### iTunes

Traditionally, the main way to add photos is to sync them through iTunes.

1. Connect your iPad to the computer, via USB cable or wirelessly, and click iTunes. Your iPad will show in the top bar. Click this and select the Photos tab.

2. Make sure there's a check mark beside Sync Photos from, then click on the drop-down menu to choose your picture library, such as iPhoto.

**Step 2:** Check Sync Photos and then choose the library you wish to sync from the options displayed.

3. It's unlikely that you'll want to sync all your photos to the iPad or have sufficient space. So click Selected albums, Events and Faces, and automatically include no Events, then go through the list of Albums and select the ones to sync.

4. When finished, click Apply or Sync.

## Hot Tip

As you select each photo album, keep an eye on the Capacity bar underneath. This will change, indicating how big it is and the amount of free space left.

# SHARING PHOTOS

**The iPad is a great digital hub for collecting, managing and adding special effects to your photos before sharing them online.**

## iCLOUD PHOTO STREAM

Copy your photos to Apple's online storage service, iCloud, and they can be automatically pushed out and received wirelessly on your computer (Mac and PC) or iOS devices. The beauty of iCloud is that it is built in to your apps, so it works silently in the background. To set up iCloud, *see page 100.*

### Sharing Your Photo Stream

Share individual pictures from your Photo Stream with friends and family you choose.

### Hot Tip

iCloud provides unlimited free storage for music and apps, etc. that you buy through iTunes, as well as for your Photo Stream. However, there's only 5GB of free storage for your documents, mail, other photos and backups, although you can purchase more space as needed.

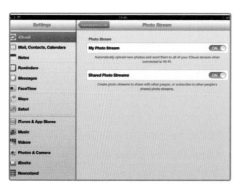

**Step 1:** Activate Shared Photo Streams by toggling the switch to On in the Photo Stream section of iCloud settings.

1. First, tap Settings, iCloud, Photo Stream and turn on Shared Photo Streams.

2. Open the Photos app, tap Photo Stream, then the Edit button. Select the photo(s) you want to show off to others and tap the Share button in the top-left corner.

3. In the pop-up window write the email address of the person you're sharing it with or tap the + sign with the blue background to select from your Contacts list.

4.  Give it a name and select whether you want anyone to be able to browse this shared photo stream via iCloud.com, then tap Next. Add a comment if desired and click Done.

5.  If your contacts use iOS 6 or later, they can see the shared photo stream in the Photos app or iPhoto app on the Mac if it runs the latest operating system, Mountain Lion.

6.  If not, it's still possible for them to view the photo albums directly on iCloud.com, but they will need an Apple ID.

# SHARING DIRECT FROM YOUR iPAD

To make it easier to share your photos, via text, email or social media, all the different options have been brought together under one Share button.

## Photos App

There are several ways to share images from the built-in Photos app. Tap to open it, select the image to share and press the Share button – a square box with pointing arrow.

- **Mail:** Tap this to open a new email message with the photo already attached. The photo has automatically been reduced in size to save space.

- **Message:** Again, the photo is automatically added to your message. All you need do is add the contact address, your message and press Send.

- **Photo Stream:** Press this to add a photo that wasn't taken with the iPad's built-in cameras to your stream of the most recent images stored on iCloud.

**Above:** Share your photos by tapping the Share icon in the top right corner. Choose how you want to share your image from the options shown, which include sharing via Facebook, Twitter and Email.

- **Twitter:** Tap the icon and a Tweet box opens with a thumbnail of the photo attached by paper clip. Notice that the number of characters left for your message has been reduced from the normal 140. This is to allow for the link to the page where the image will be stored.

- **Facebook:** Posting a photo to the world's biggest social network is also incredibly easy. Tap the Facebook icon and the picture is already attached. Underneath is the name of the Facebook album to which the photo will be added. To change this, tap the name and select a different album from the pop-up box.

# ONLINE ALBUMS

Move your pictures from the iPad to online photo-sharing sites such as Flickr and Google's Picasa or create your own web gallery using Journals.

**Above:** The Picasa Web Albums HD app lets you access your Picasa photo library online, and and post photos to Google+.

## Picasa

As well as being an online photo-sharing site in its own right, Picasa, which is owned by Google, is also used to create the photo albums in Google's social network, Google+. There are third-party apps, such as Web Albums HD, which let you access your entire Picasa photo library online, as well as post to Google+.

**Hot Tip**

If you want to set up and view albums only on Google+ itself, there is a Google+ app available in iTunes.

## Flickr

As it's one of the biggest online photo-sharing sites, several photo-editing apps, such as iPhoto, let you post directly to Flickr. In addition, there are many third-party apps, such as FlickStackr, for bringing Flickr photo-sharing to the iPad. This allows you to upload and download photos, add information to the photo, and view Flickr groups and discussions.

# PHOTO SERVICES

Get creative with your iPad and use your photos to create online journals, greeting cards and much more.

## Journals

Using iPhoto, you can create your own photo journal and display it on the web through iCloud or your own website if you have one. Select the photos you want, add maps, dates, weather icons and notes.

## Photobooks

Apps such as eBook Magic take your photos – including pictures taken with your iPad camera – and turn them into photo albums, story books for your children or travel journals.

## Greeting Cards

Surprise gran with a greeting card featuring the family. Apps such as Greetings Studio let you incorporate photos from the iPad into a series of templates to create personalized cards for all occasions.

**Above:** Turn your photos into jigsaw puzzles by downloading the Jigsawed Jigsaw Puzzle app.

## Calendars

Make your holiday last a year. InstaCalendar for the iPad will let you memorialize your trip by turning your travel shots – or any photo – into a calendar.

## Puzzles

Jigsawed Jigsaw Puzzle turns your photos into jigsaws – ranging from 9 pieces if it's for the children to 324 for the more experienced.

# YOUR VIDEOS

Shooting and editing video is so easy on the iPad that you will soon be creating movie clips to share on the internet. Go viral, and your clip could be the latest online sensation.

## VIDEO RECORDING

Point and tap is all you need to do to start recording your video, provided you've got an iPad 2 or later, but there are a few things to bear in mind in order to get the best results.

### Shooting Video

The video recorder is built in to the Camera app you use to take photos.

1.  To start, simply tap the Camera app and slide the switch in the bottom-right corner to video.

2.  Point the camera at the scene you want to capture and tap the recording button in the centre-right of the screen.

3.  A bell sound marks the start of recording and the red dot in the middle of the camera icon starts flashing. A timer showing how long you've been recording appears in the top-right corner.

4.  To finish recording, tap the record button again. Watch your movie clip by tapping the video library icon in the bottom-left corner.

**Step 2**: Start recording your video by tapping the red recording button to the centre-right of the screen.

## Focusing Your Video Recording

While the iPad has its own autofocus, you can target a particular area. Tap the screen, and a white box appears. Point the camera, so this box covers the area you want highlighted.

## Which Video Camera to Use

The iPad has come with two cameras since the iPad 2.

- **The front-facing camera**: Primarily intended for FaceTime video chat calls, this has a lower resolution than the rear camera. If you do want to use the front camera – perhaps to introduce your clip – switch lenses by tapping the camera icon with two circular arrows on the bottom menu.

- **The rear camera**: The default one for video. The iPad 2 has a 0.7-megapixel lens that shoots video at 720p. On later iPads this iSight camera has been upgraded massively to a 5-megapixel lens, which shoots full 1080p HD (high-definition) video. It also includes a clever auto-stabilization feature to compensate for any shakiness when filming.

### Hot Tip

Although you can view your video equally well in portrait or landscape mode, choose one or the other before you begin and don't switch midway through filming.

# EDITING VIDEO

Tidy up your video by using the Camera app to trim unwanted footage from the beginning and end of your clip – or use iMovie for more extensive movie-editing.

## Simple Editing

1.  Once you've shot your video, tap the Camera Roll in the bottom-left corner to view the clip.

**Step 2**: Tap the screen to show a timeline of your video, with the cursor marking where you are in the clip.

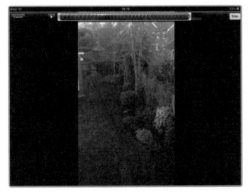

**Step 6**: Tap the Trim button and then choose between Trim Original and Save as New Clip.

## Hot Tip
It's best to have your iPad in horizontal view when running iMovie as you can see more of your timeline and the editing controls.

2.   If the top bar is not visible, tap the screen so it appears. In the middle is a timeline of your video, with the cursor showing where you are in the clip.

3.   Around the timeline is a grey border with a handle at either end. Press one of these, and the border will turn yellow.

4.   Drag the left handle to the right to trim the start of the video, or the right handle to the left to alter the end.

5.   Hold your finger down on one of the handles to zoom in and place your end point more precisely.

6.   Tap the Trim button. Select Trim Original, and the existing video clip is replaced by the trimmed version. Tap Save as New Clip and both versions are kept.

## More Advanced Movie Editing
With Apple's iMovie app (purchased through the App Store) on the iPad, you have many of the video-editing features available in the full version of the program that runs on your computer.

## Import Video
The iMovie app lets you polish up your video footage, combine clips, and add titles and special effects in the transitions between scenes.

1. Open iMovie, tap the + button, then New Project to create a new folder for your video.

2. Grant iMovie permission to access your photos. To add other videos, tap the filmstrip icon, where you should see the most recent video clip you recorded. Tap this and then the blue downward-pointing arrow to add it to your timeline.

3. Tap the Photos icon to access your photo library. As well as any video clips you have, you can also add photos. In fact, several copies of the photo are added so that it lasts on screen for about three to six seconds. There are also slight variations to give the effect that the camera is zooming in on the scene. Tap the photo you want, and it will be added to the end of the timeline.

**Step 3**: Add a photo from your photo library to the end of your timeline. Multiple copies are added so the photo lasts on screen.

4. Alternatively, capture video direct from within iMovie by tapping the video camera icon. This accesses the iPad's iSight camera and you can shoot your HD video as before.

5. The red vertical line, known as the playhead, shows where you are in the video. The image by the playhead is displayed in the preview window above.

6. Flick your finger left or right to scroll through the timeline. Pinch your fingers to zoom in and out or press the triangular Play button under the preview window to start the video.

## Edit Video

Having added the video clips to your project, you can edit them into your personal blockbuster movie.

○ **Rearrange a clip**: To change the order in which they play, tap-and-hold the clip you're moving and drag it to the new location. The existing clips move to make space.

○ **Delete a clip**: Double-tap the clip you want to remove, and select Delete Clip in the box that opens. If you change your mind and want to add it back, it will still be in the list of available video clips.

**Above**: Delete a clip by double-tapping and selecting Delete Clip.

○ **Trim a clip**: This is done in much the same way as in the Camera app. Tap the clip in the timeline and then drag the yellow endpoints to a new start and finish position.

○ **Split a clip**: Tap the clip you want, and drag it until the playhead is right over the spot where you want to split it. Tap the video, and it will be outlined in yellow. Swipe your finger down the playhead as though you were slicing it in half. Now you can add another clip or insert a different transition.

## Edit Transitions

The on-screen move from one clip to the next is called a transition. There are three types.

○ **Cut transition**: Marked by a white line on a black square this is called None in iMovie because, although there is a break between clips, there's no transition effect. On screen, one clip will just flow into the next but the transition will still be shown in the timeline in case you want to change it.

○ **Theme transition**: Marked by two white boxes on a black background. To choose the theme to apply, tap the Project Settings button – the cog wheel – in the top-right corner and make your choice.

- **Cross-Dissolve transition**: Shown by two triangles pointing at each other, lets one clip fade into the other.

## Select Transitions

By default, there's a transition between each video clip and photo in the project.

1. To change it, double-tap the transition icon in the timeline.

2. In the Transition Settings window that opens select the style you want. To change how long it lasts, tap the duration required.

3. Tap on the yellow triangles below the transition button to open the precision editor. This lets you move the endpoints where you want the transition to begin and end. Tap the triangles to return to the timeline.

> **Hot Tip**
>
> If Cross-Dissolve isn't available, it's because the clips either side aren't long enough to support it.

**Step 3:** Tap the yellow triangles below the transition button to open the precision editor.

## Add Titles

Another way to give a more professional finish to your videos is to overlay titles.

1. Double-tap the clip and in the Settings box that opens select Title Style. Choose the style and see how it will look in the preview area.

2. Tap the text box and use the on-screen keyboard to add your title.

3. On some themes you can add a location. Tap Location and enter the details or select the Crosshairs icon to add it automatically.

# ADDING SOUND TO YOUR VIDEO

From recording your own commentary to adding a song from your iTunes collection, there are several ways to add sound to your video.

## Background Music

If you are adventurous, you can record your own music with an app like GarageBand; you can also select iMovie theme music or add any song from your iTunes library.

1. To add music, tap the Audio button (musical notes icon), then Theme Music.

2. Only one music track can play at a time. If you add a music track when there is already one in place, it will play after this if the video is long enough. If it's not it will replace the original music.

**Step 1**: Tap the musical notes icon and select Theme Music to begin adding background music to your videos.

3. If you have background music looping turned on (that is the track keeps repeating throughout the video) then you can only have one track. If you want more than one you have to turn this off.

4. To turn music looping on or off, tap the Project Settings button (gear wheel icon) in the upper-right of the screen and select the appropriate option.

5. To set the volume of the background music tap the Waveform button in the middle bar and you'll see a mix of yellow and red peaks. Red shows the audio is too loud and likely to be distorted.

6. Change the volume until these peaks disappear, by double-tapping the green background in the timeline that represents the audio clip and adjusting the slider.

## Sound Effects

Add these at relevant points by scrolling through the timeline so the playhead is where you want to add the sound effect. Tap the Audio button and then Sound effects. Preview a sound by tapping the Play button on the right. It will be shown as a blue bar in the timeline. Adjust the volume by double-tapping this and then moving the slider.

## Backing Track

When you record the video, it might include all sorts of background noises or conversations. If the clip does have its own audio, iMovie will automatically lower the volume (known as audio ducking) of the background music.

## Voiceover

Place the red-line playhead where you want

**Step 5**: Set the volume of your background music by tapping the Waveform button and using the slider to change the volume until any red peaks disappear.

**Above:** After recording your voiceover you can choose whether to review it, retake it, cancel it or accept it.

to start recording and then tap the microphone icon. Tap Record in the pop-up box and after a three-second countdown, start talking. Press the Stop button to finish recording. You then have the options to Review the voiceover, Retake, Cancel or Accept it.

# SHARE YOUR VIDEOS

Once you have the perfect movie, the iPad makes it simple to share your video with friends, family or the wider world of the internet, via YouTube and Facebook.

### Sharing from the Camera Roll
Tap the Share button in the Camera Roll and select your preferred option.

- **Email**: There will be a slight delay while the video is compressed to reduce the size of the file that's sent. Because this also reduces the quality of the video, do not use email to send the video to your computer – it's better to sync them using iTunes.

- **Message**: The video is automatically attached, so you just have to add who it's going to and write your message.

- **YouTube**: This is the best option to display your video properly. Enter your sign-in details in the pop-up box and then add a title, description, tags and category for your video.

### Sharing from iMovie
1. When you've finished, tap the iMovie icon on the top bar and you'll return to the Home screen. If you haven't given the project a name, do so now. Tap My Project and enter the title you prefer. Tap the Share button and you'll see the range of options available.

2. Most links are to well-known video-sharing sites, such as YouTube, Facebook,

## Hot Tip
By default your video is uploaded in standard definition. Select HD if you want high definition. As the file size is much bigger, it will take longer to upload, so you should only do this over a Wi-Fi connection to the internet rather than mobile.

Vimeo and CNNiReport. You will need to have an account for the site you select before you can upload your video.

**Step 1:** Tap the Share button in the iMovie Home screen to view and select how you want to share your video from the options shown.

3. The procedure is typically the same: enter your login details and then complete the form for your video. It should include a title, a description and the category under which it should be displayed. In addition you can choose the file size.

4. Some sites also let you set who can see the video through the privacy settings. There may be some videos that you want to share only with the family or friends, but, generally, if you want your video to be seen, it's best to go public.

**Hot Tip**

If you do go public on a video-sharing site, make sure you have the permission of anyone featured in it and you have copyright for the material used.

5. You can also send the video to your Camera Roll for emailing or add it to iTunes, so it can be synced with your Mac or PC.

# ENTERTAINMENT CENTRE

Whether it's a Hollywood blockbuster or must-see TV series, it can be bought or rented to view in glorious detail on your iPad – or to project onto your TV.

## AIRPLAY

AirPlay lets you wirelessly transmit videos and other content from your iPad to the big screen – and show them on your TV.

### Apple TV

As well as streaming what's on your iPad – music, photos and so on – Apple TV also lets you show content on the big screen from Netflix, YouTube and Vimeo, plus films and TV shows from the iTunes store and more.

1. To mirror the screen of your iPad on the TV wirelessly, you will need the second generation Apple TV and an iPad 2 or later.

   **Above:** The Apple TV black box connects to your TV and wirelessly receives video streams from your iPad.

   This black box is physically connected to your TV by High Density Multimedia Interface (HDMI) cable and wirelessly receives the video stream from your iPad, using AirPlay mirroring.

2. To work successfully, both your iPad and Apple TV have to be on the same Wi-Fi network.

3. Turn on AirPlay on your Apple TV. Using the remote supplied with it, navigate the on-screen display on your TV and select Settings, Airplay and turn it on.

4.  Double-tap the Home button on your iPad to access the open app list. Flick to the right and you'll see the media controls.

5.  Select AirPlay and then tap the Apple TV you want to use to mirror the iPad.

## Physical Connection to Your TV

For a less flexible approach to mirroring what's on your iPad screen to a TV or other display, you can cable the two together.

**Step 4**: Double-tap the Home button on your iPad. Flick right and select the AirPlay icon from the media controls, and then tap Apple TV.

## View Rented Movies through Your Apple TV

Once Apple TV is set up, you should see the iTunes Store, which lets you access the same video and TV shows available through the iPad.

1.  Select Movies from the main Apple TV menu. Browse through the different options – top movies, Genius recommendations, film genres or individual titles.

2.  When you see a movie you want to rent, select it. With the second- and third-generation Apple TV it will default to the high-definition version of the film (which will take longer to download and will be more expensive).

3.  To change this preference go to Settings, iTunes store, then Video Resolution and change from the two HD formats 1080p or 720p to Standard Definition (SD). In fact, the 1080p movies will only play on the third generation Apple TV.

4.  A confirmation message will appear on screen. Click OK if you want to continue, and the film will download. A message appears when it is ready to view. Press Play to start watching.

5.  If you rent a movie through Apple
    TV, it can be viewed only through
    Apple TV.

## Buy and Rent Videos through the iTunes Store

1.  Tap the iTunes app to access the store
    and select the Film tab at the bottom.

2.  You can select from Featured movies, which shows you the most popular films to rent or
    buy, as well as recommendations from iTunes. Alternatively, select Charts and you can see
    the top movies in each category.

3.  By default, all types of movie are shown in both the Featured and Charts section. If you
    have a specific taste in film, such as horror, tap the Genres button and make your selection
    – then, just those movies will be shown.

**Above:** Select the Film tab at the bottom of the iTunes app to view movies available for renting and purchase.

4.  When you see a movie you want to
    rent, select it. You'll see Details of the
    film, including a trailer, synopsis and
    cast list. At the top is the overall
    rating from iTunes users and the price
    to buy or rent the movie.

5.  To see more detailed opinions about
    the film – and add your own once
    you've seen it – tap the Reviews tab.

6.  If it doesn't appeal, select Related
    and you'll see similar films that

customers who purchased the film you're looking at have also bought.

7. Tap the Rent button if you want to hire the movie. You'll have up to 30 days to view the film. But once you've started to watch it, you have just 24 hours to complete it.

8. Movies rented through the iPad can be viewed only on the iPad (or on the TV using AirPlay). They can't be transferred to your computer for viewing there.

**Above:** Click on a movie you are interested in to see further details and the price to buy or rent.

9. To buy a film, select the relevant button. For the iPad 3 and later, the default is to download the HD (high-definition) version of the movie. For the iPad 1 and 2 it will be the SD (standard-definition) version.

**Hot Tip**

The HD version is more expensive and a much bigger file size, so will take longer to download.

**Hot Tip**

Don't worry if you accidentally delete a TV show or movie you have bought. Go to Purchased, select Films or TV Series and locate the programme you want to re-download.

## TV Shows

TV shows operate in a similar way to the movies, except they are only available to buy. You can browse by Featured Programmes and Charts, and within each section you have the option to view single Episodes of a show or the collected Series. There are also an increasing number of TV shows that offer both HD and SD versions.

# PLAY VIDEOS

**Whether it's for the latest movie, a music clip or a converted file of the children's school play, the iPad is an immensely powerful video player.**

## MASTER VIDEO PLAYER

All the video content downloaded from the iTunes store – whether it's a movie, TV show or music video – appears automatically in the Videos app. Its distinctive icon features a movie clapperboard.

### Playback

1. Turn your iPad to switch between viewing your video in portrait or widescreen (landscape) mode.

2. Tap the Play button (forward-facing triangle) or the video itself to start playback. Press the centre button to pause playback.

**Step 4:** Navigate to your chosen point in a video by dragging your finger to move the playhead along the timeline at the top of the screen.

3. Touch and hold the Rewind or Fast Forward icon to speed backward and forward through the video.

4. Alternatively, drag the playhead along the scrubber bar (as the video timeline is called) at the top to any point of the video you want.

5. As you drag the playhead back, slide your finger down the screen to slow the scrub rate. You'll see a label that reads Hi-Speed Scrubbing, Half-Speed Scrubbing and Fine Scrubbing.

6.  To go right back to the beginning of the video, drag the playhead all the way to the left or simply tap the Rewind button (if the video has no chapters; if it does, it will go back to the beginning of the chapter).

7.  Tap the Chapters button and you'll see a list of chapters in the movie (if there are any). Tap the name to go directly to that chapter.

8.  Use the volume slider to raise or lower the soundtrack on the video.

9.  To stop the video before it finishes playing, tap the Done button or press the Home button.

## OTHER VIDEO PLAYERS

In addition to the Videos app, you can watch video on your iPad through the Safari web browser and third-party apps that connect directly to video sites.

### Video Browsing

Browse the internet and you'll see that many websites, from personal blogs to international newspapers, music and entertainment sites, include video. Virtually any video in the standard MP4 format will play on the iPad through the Safari web browser.

As with all Apple devices running iOS, no Flash videos can play on the iPad directly. The popularity of the iPad is such that this is becoming less of an issue than it was before.

**Hot Tip**

Want to know what's on the web? Clicker (www.clicker.com) claims to be the only complete directory of TV, movies and web series available online. Access it from the iPad and the videos it shows will all be iPad-compatible versions.

**Above:** Access the Clicker website from the Safari web browser to show all iPad-compatible TV shows and movies.

Rather than lose a portion of their audience, many sites are changing the format for their videos so they can run on the iPad. There are also browsers, like Skyfire, that do this conversion in the background so Flash videos will play on the iPad. It doesn't have a 100 per cent success rate, though.

## Video Apps

There are several video sites that have their own apps for the iPad. Netflix and LOVEFiLM both have apps for subscribers to their service, as do Amazon and Hulu in the US with its Instant Video app. Typically, for a monthly subscription you can access any of the vast library of movies and TV shows these sites hold.

## Video-sharing Sites

The popularity of YouTube was such that their app was built-in to the iPad's operating system, but Apple removed the YouTube app in iOS 6.

Instead, there is a standalone app, which you can download from the App Store. Another popular video-sharing site, Vimeo, has its own dedicated app for the iPad, while Blip (blip.tv) offers professionally made shows that run as 'web series', viewable through Safari on the iPad.

## TV Sites

Many TV companies have developed apps – such as BBC iPlayer and Sky Go – that let you watch programmes on the iPad, sometimes live. Other companies have optimized their websites, so it's now possible to play back previous episodes of their shows through the iPad.

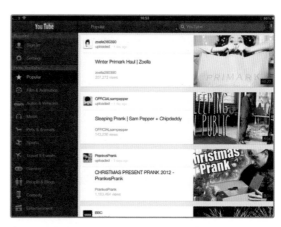

**Above:** YouTube is a popular video sharing site, which can be accessed through a dedicated iPad app.

# STREAMING MEDIA/VIDEO

Most videos are streamed to your iPad via your internet connection, so you can start watching within a few minutes, rather than wait for it to download completely.

**Above:** Stream programmes from BBC iPlayer to start watching them within minutes.

- **Streaming**: with streaming, just a small amount of data is downloaded to the iPad. This is a buffer against any interruption caused by any slowdown or delay on the internet connection that could affect your viewing.

- **Buffering**: while the movie is being buffered, you see a circular, revolving line. If the film is regularly halting and the buffering icon appears, it is because of problems with the internet connection.

- **Bandwidth**: streaming video naturally takes up a lot of bandwidth. The higher the quality of the movie, the more bandwidth it needs. For example, Netflix has three levels – Good, which is up to 0.3 GB/hour; Better, which is up to 0.7 GB/hour; Best, which is about 1 GB/hour. However, if you're viewing the movie in high definition (HD), this shoots up to 2.3 GB/hour.

## Hot Tip

If you are having problems viewing a streaming video, the first thing to do is choose a lower quality setting.

- **Viewing Problems**: in addition to how much bandwidth you have, streaming can be affected by other factors, such as the amount of other traffic, if you're sharing the connection, or interference from other wireless products.

# SYNC VIDEOS

**Having shot your video masterpiece or purchased the latest film release, you need to make sure it's available on the iPad in a format that will work.**

## iTUNES

Use iTunes to keep the videos on your computer and iPad in sync – or to share access to videos without having to transfer them first.

○ Once you purchase a TV show or movie from iTunes, it will automatically download to your iPad. The next time you sync your iPad with your computer, it will be moved to your iTunes library on your computer.

○ Through iCloud, it can also be automatically downloaded to other iOS devices that use the same iTunes account.

**Step 3**: Choose Videos from the iPad settings menu and enter your Apple ID and password under the Home Sharing title.

### Home Sharing

Instead of transferring the movies to your iPad, you can play them from your Mac or PC over your Wi-Fi network.

1.  To play videos from your iTunes library on Mac or PC to your iPad, you have to make sure they are both on the same home network.

2.  Open iTunes on your computer and in the File menu choose Home Sharing and then Turn On Home Sharing. Enter your Apple ID and password and click Turn On Home Sharing.

3.  Tap Settings on the iPad and choose Videos; under Home sharing enter the same Apple ID.

4.  Now launch the Videos app and you'll see there's a new tab, Shared. Select a shared library; there may be several if you are sharing iTunes on different computers.

5.  Tap the Library you want, select the type of video you want – Movies, TV Shows or Music Videos – and then choose the one you want to play.

# CONVERT VIDEOS TO iPAD-FRIENDLY FORMAT

The iPad supports only a limited number of video formats. While movies and TV shows downloaded from the iTunes store and services such as Netflix will usually be iPad compatible, there are many that may not be, including your own home movies.

## Convert Using iTunes

You can use iTunes to convert video into an iPad-friendly format. Add the video to iTunes by going to File, Add to Library and selecting the video file. Once you have imported it, select the video and in the File menu select Create New Version and then Create iPad or Apple TV version.

**Above:** You can download the Video Converter app for iPad.

## Convert Using Third-party Apps

There are many third-party applications – free and paid for – that will make conversion quick and easy. Some, like Wondershare's Video Converter Ultimate, will optimize your video for playback on the iPad and, once the conversion is done, automatically add it to your iTunes library for syncing with the iPad.

### Hot Tip

You may have to be patient if you use iTunes to convert your home movie. The results are not always great and, depending on how long your movie is, conversion can take a long time.

READING

# iBOOKS

**Through this free reader, you can read books on the iPad, whether they're downloaded from iBookstore, Apple's online bookshop, or elsewhere on the internet.**

## BUILDING UP YOUR BOOK COLLECTION

With hundreds of thousands of free and paid-for books in iBookstore, there's plenty of choice available.

### iBookstore

The book store is accessed from within the iBooks app, which is available as a free download from the App Store.

1. Once it's installed, tap iBooks. When it opens for the first time, you'll see a set of empty wooden bookshelves, ready to hold your books. Tap the Store button in the top-left corner, which opens iBookstore.

2. In reality this just opens the Books section of the iTunes store. To look through the store, just select a relevant button. You can see featured titles, charts of the most popular and so on.

**Above:** Browse the iBookstore by scrolling through, or search by category using the buttons displayed in the tool bar.

3. To filter the list of available titles, tap the All Categories button at the top of the page and select which genre you are most interested in, such as Crime & Thrillers, Food & Drink, etc.

4.  If you know what you're looking for use the Search box. You can also tap the Browse button with its icon of a pair of spectacles (Top Authors on the iPad mini) and search by author's name, choosing between paid-for works and free.

5.  Tap the book cover and the information box opens with all the details to help you decide if it's one you want to read. As well as the standard book information about the publisher, author, price and so on, there is a Sample button, which lets you read a short extract from the book.

6.  Below this is a more detailed description of the book, ratings and reviews by other iBookstore users and links to related titles.

# DOWNLOAD BOOKS

Whether it's through iBookstore or the web, there is a variety of ways you can build up your personal library on your iPad.

## From the iBookstore

1.  Choice made, tap the price or Free button, then Get Book. You may be prompted to confirm your purchase or enter your password for your Apple ID.

2.  The iBookstore spins round to show your iBooks bookshelves. The title being downloaded is shown in the top shelf with a progress bar at the bottom of the book.

3.  Once the book is downloaded, tap the cover to open it and start reading. *See page 135 for more details.*

## Internet

iBooks supports two of the most popular ebook formats, EPUB (electronic publication) and PDF (portable document format). You can find books in these formats all over the web; for example,

**Above:** Visit the epubbooks.com website to browse titles and download them to iBooks.

**Step 1:** Once downloaded you can choose to open your new book in iBooks.

from Project Gutenberg (www.gutenberg.org), epubBooks (www.epubbooks.com) or ManyBooks.net.

1.  To download these books directly to iBooks, open Safari and go to the site. Select the book you want, choose one of the two formats above (if available) and tap the Download link. On sites such as ManyBooks.net you can then choose to Open in 'iBooks'.

2.  Similarly, if you receive an ebook or link to one in your email, tap it and it will be added to iBooks.

3.  Alternatively, if you have already downloaded the ebooks to your computer, you can transfer them to iBooks on your iPad, via iTunes. Just drag the EPUB book file into your iTunes library on the computer (or select Add to Library from the File menu in iTunes and choose the file). When you sync your iPad with the computer, the ebook will be transferred to one of the shelves in iBooks.

## Hot Tip

There is a third format that iBooks supports – interactive textbooks, where the text includes images, sounds, videos, animations and even 3D objects. These are made using a special Apple format and are available only in the iBookstore.

## Automatic Downloading via iCloud

All the books you buy from iBookstore will appear in your iBooks library but are actually stored in iCloud, Apple's online storage and backup service. This means that if you purchased a book on your computer or iPhone, you can download and read it on your iPad.

- ⊙ **Purchased:** If it's a book you've already purchased, tap the Purchased icon at the bottom of the iBookstore screen. Tap the Cloud icon beside the book you want to download.

- ⊙ **Sync Books:** In order to automatically sync books purchased across all your iDevices, tap Settings, then iTunes & App Stores and turn on Books in the Automatic Downloads section.

# ORGANIZE YOUR BOOKS

In every library, there are times when you need to sort out your book collection, remove some and make the ones you use frequently more accessible. iBooks makes that simple.

## Remove the Shelves

While the virtual bookshelves appeal to some, others find them irritating. For a more traditional list view, tap the button with three white lines on the right of the toolbar.

**Above:** You can remove the virtual bookshelves to display your books in a more traditional list view.

## Rearrange Your Books

- ⊙ **In Bookshelf View:** Tap the Edit button, and then touch and hold the book until it zooms out, and place it in a new position.

- ⊙ **In List View:** Tap the Edit button in the top-right corner and then drag the book, using the grabber handles, to a new position in the list.

## Hot Tip

You can also sort books in list view using the buttons at the bottom, so that they are displayed by title, author or category.

## Delete Books

- **To delete a book**: Tap the Edit button and select one or more books. A white tick mark will appear on each one chosen. Tap the Delete button to remove the books, then Done.

- **In List View**: You can also delete a book by swiping your finger from right to left and tapping the Delete button that appears.

## Book Collections

If you've got a series of books on a particular subject that interests you, group them into a collection.

**Above:** All new downloads are assigned to a pre-set collection, but you can also create a New collection.

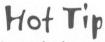

## Hot Tip

You can back up your collections, so they can be restored if anything goes wrong. Tap Settings, iBooks and turn on **Sync Collections**.

- **Pre-set Collections**: iBooks comes with three pre-set collections: Books, Purchased Books and PDFs.

- **Libraries**: Collections are shown in separate libraries. To switch between them, tap the Collections button and select the one you want.

- **New Collection**: To add your own group of books, tap Collections, and then New, and write in a name. Go to the collections that currently house the books. Tap the Edit button, select the titles you want in the new collection and press the Move button. Select the new collection and the ebooks will be moved there.

- **Delete a Collection**: To delete a collection, tap the Collections button, select the one you want from the list, tap the Edit button and press Delete. Deleting a collection also removes all the books in it.

# READERS

The lightness of the iPad, and the iPad mini in particular, gives it a natural advantage for reading books – especially when it can also hold most of your library.

## eBOOK READERS

Most ebook readers work in a similar way. Apple iBooks, shown below, allows you to bookmark pages and write notes, and will remember where you last finished reading.

### Reading on the iPad

1. Open iBooks and tap the cover of the book you want to read. If you have already started reading a book, iBooks will automatically open at the last page you read.

2. Generally, if you hold the iPad in portrait view, there'll be one page to a screen. In landscape view there will be two pages.

3. To turn a page, tap the screen on the right and flick left. To turn the page back, tap the left of the screen and flick to the right.

4. As you read, there's nothing on the page to distract your attention. To access the Reading controls at the top of the page and the Page Navigator at the bottom, touch the middle of the page. To close them, touch the page again.

**Step 4:** When you read on an iPad there are no reading controls which may distract you. To access them, touch the middle of the page.

## Navigating the Book

- **Library button**: Takes you back to the bookshelf or list view of your books.

- **Contents button**: Tap this to jump to the Contents section. Scroll through the list of what's in the book and tap any of the headings to go direct to that page. Tap the button, now labelled Resume, to return to where you were.

- **Move to a page**: Drag the slider at the bottom of the page. As you move across, there's a text box with the Chapter heading and page numbers. When you let go, the book will open at that page. Alternatively, tap the magnifying glass icon and type the page number in the box.

- **Revisit a page**: Use the Go to Page XX link or Back to Page XX link at the bottom of the screen.

## Hot Tip

You can also turn a page by tapping the left or right margin. To activate this feature tap Settings, iBooks and turn on Both Margins Advance.

**Above:** Navigate through your iBooks by touching the screen to show control icons such as bookmarks, contents, and the slider at the bottom of the page.

## Bookmarks

If there's a particularly notable passage in the book that you know you'll want to revisit, bookmark it. Tap the bookmark icon in the far right corner. You can access all your bookmarks at any time by tapping the Contents icon and selecting Bookmarks.

## Notes

Highlight a key passage or add a note by tapping-and-holding any word. Use the endpoints to choose the exact content you want. Then use the pop-up menu to do the following.

- **Copy**: Then paste into a document you're working on – handy if you want to add a reference to an essay or review.

- **Define**: This shows not only the word's meaning but also how it is used and other words that are derived from it.

- **Highlight**: This opens several other options, including a choice of highlight colour, adding a note or switching to underlining.

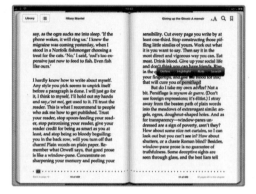

**Above:** Tap and hold to highlight a word or phrase, and choose from options to copy, define and so on.

- **Note**: This opens the same yellow note box you can choose in the highlighting options. Add your comments using the on-screen keyboard. As with bookmarks, you can access all your notes by tapping the Contents button and then selecting Notes. To delete a note, just remove all the text in it.

- **Share**: Bizarrely, the first time you choose this iBooks will ask permission to access your Photos app. This is because it is the same Share box that appears, with options to add the highlighted quote to an email, text message, Tweet or Facebook update.

## Changing Appearance

Unlike the printed book, with iBooks you can adjust the text and layout of your ebook to make it more comfortable for reading. Tap the letter A icon.

- **Screen brightness**: use the slider to adjust.

- **Font size**: Tap the smaller letter A to reduce the size of the text and the larger one to increase it.

### Hot Tip

Back up your bookmarks and notes, so you do not lose them and can also access them on any other iDevice you use to read the book. Tap Settings, iBooks and turn on Sync Bookmarks.

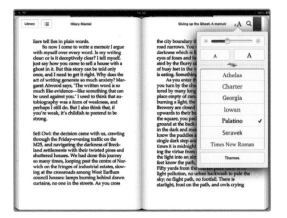

**Above:** Tap the aA button to improve readability by adjusting font choice and size.

- **Fonts:** Choose the font that offers the best readability.

- **Themes:** Change the background colour. Remove the virtual book imagery by tapping Full Screen or read the book as one continuous page by pressing Scroll.

- **Justified text:** If you find it easier to read a book in which the text is evenly spaced across the line, go to Settings, iBooks and switch on Full Justification.

## Searching Text

Tap the magnifying glass icon at the top of the page and type in the word or phrase you are looking for. All references to it that are found are displayed in the text box below. To widen your search to look on the Web or in Wikipedia, the online encyclopedia to which anyone can contribute, tap the relevant button.

## Read Aloud

Save your energy when reading stories aloud and have the iPad narrate the tale for you. iBooks can read stories aloud using the VoiceOver screen reader that aids accessibility to the iPad for visually impaired users.

## Read Aloud

1. To find a Read aloud storybook, tap Store in iBooks and then type Read aloud in the Search bar.

2. Tap the chosen book to open it and then the loudspeaker icon on the top menu. Under Read aloud select pages to turn Automatically and then tap Start Reading.

3. The storyteller starts and the text is highlighted word by word.

4. To move to any page, use the scrub bar at the bottom, which has tiny thumbnails showing where you are in the book. (If it's not visible, tap the middle of the page.) Slide your finger along the bar to the place you want and tap the word you want to start from, and the story will continue from there.

5. To pause reading at any point, tap the loudspeaker icon again and then Stop Reading.

**Above:** After downloading a read aloud book tap the loudspeaker icon on the top menu. You can then select pages to turn automatically and tap Start Reading.

# OTHER BOOKSTORES

There are several rival online bookstores, such as Google Play Books and Amazon's Kindle Store, for which you'll need different apps.

## Hot Tip

With Read aloud editions of books, words are highlighted as they are spoken by the narrator, which is a real boon for youngsters learning to read.

### Google Play

This is Google's alternative to the iTunes store. Primarily aimed at those who use Android devices (which rival Apple's iOS devices), its books can be read on the iPad through the Google Play Books app, available from the App Store.

Google claim their bookstore has the world's largest selection of ebooks, including millions of free titles, but because of Apple's policies you can't shop for new titles direct from the app. Instead, you have to access the store through Safari (or your iPad or your computer) and purchase the titles you want online. They will then automatically appear in the Google Play Books app, so you can read them. The book controls are similar to those in iBooks and you can download the books for reading offline, when you have no internet connection.

## Kindle

Kindle for iPad is the free reading app from the Amazon bookstore. There are more than one million free and paid-for Kindle books available. As with Google Play Books, you have to get your titles online. Amazon's whispersync technology can then sync the book with any computers and iDevices that have the Kindle app. To save space on your iPad, you can store the bulk of your books in the Amazon cloud, only downloading the books that you want to read on the iPad.

As with iBooks, you can create Collections, which group your books into related areas of interest. Once you start reading the book, the last page read, bookmarks, notes and highlights will also all be synced, so wherever you are reading, you'll be able to start just where you left off.

**Above:** Save space by storing your Kindle books in the Amazon cloud and then downloading them to your iPad when you want to read them.

# NEWS

No more drying out the paper that's got wet, or reading across a page that's torn or wrinkled: the iPad is the perfect paper boy.

## NEWSPAPER SUBSCRIPTIONS

The iPad offers the flexibility to subscribe to your favourite daily newspaper or just buy one-off editions covering momentous events; several publishers refresh news content throughout the day.

### Newsstand Subscriptions

Originally, most newspaper iPad editions were standalone apps. However, publishers are increasingly adding their titles to Newsstand, as it enables them to auto-renew subscriptions. For more details on using Newsstand, *see* page 146.

**Above:** Subscribing to the Mail Online allows you to update content and stay up-to-date.

### Standalone Subscriptions

For publishers, the benefit of having a separate app for the newspaper is that it gives more freedom over pricing and content. Some, like the *Daily Mail*, offer a fixed version of their printed newspaper through Newsstand while having a standalone app for the iPad that's linked to their website. There are various in-app subscriptions available with the benefit that you can update the content as often as you like, so you always have the latest news.

## Tablet-only Newspaper

The *Daily* was the first newspaper created solely for the iPad and other tablets. As such, it took advantage of the iPad's dazzling display to present news, entertainment and sport in a striking way.

However, the pioneering venture was not financially sustainable in the long run, although it is likely to open the way for more digital-only news publications, like *Newsweek* – with premium content specifically designed for the iPad.

## Create Your Own Newspaper

If you prefer to be your own editor, try Early Edition 2. Redesigned to take advantage of the Retina screen, it is a news reader (and can sync with your Google Reader account) that dynamically lays out the content in a newspaper format.

As with any newspaper, stories are positioned according to the importance of their content. You can also pre-load images when you have Wi-Fi coverage, so you can carry on reading your newspaper offline, when you have no connection, such as on a flight.

**Above:** Download the Dilbert Mobile app to access the cartoons archive collection.

## Cartoons

There are celebrated newspaper cartoons available – without the newspapers. Dilbert Mobile is free (as in no charge) when downloaded from the App Store and even gives you access to the 20+ year archive of the entire collection of office-life humour.

### Hot Tip

The best of the magazine and newspaper apps are customized to take advantage of the iPad, so will have a completely different look and feel from the newspaper, with unique navigation and interactive features such as video, music and live links on the page.

# RSS FEEDS

Subscribe to a news site's RSS feed and
you can keep up with breaking news and get regular story updates. All you need is an RSS
news feed reader (also known as a news reader) for the iPad.

**Above:** Once you have downloaded a news app, select feeds you want to subscribe to by tapping the + button and then Add Feed and then Done.

## Using a News Reader

There are several news readers available in the App Store, including Feeddler, Pulse and NewsRack.

Most websites today, whether it's a blog, news site, online magazine or entertainment site, will have an RSS feed. RSS stands for Really Simple Syndication and is the standard way for websites to publish the latest news and updates.

## Adding a News Source

NewsRack is shown here, but most readers work in a similar way.

1.  Once you have downloaded and installed NewsRack, tap to launch it. If you use Google Reader as your online news reader, then you have the option to log in and sync with NewsRack.

2.  Alternatively, you can use NewsRack as a standalone reader. Press the Edit button and then the + button. Enter the website's name – such as NewYorkTimes.com – in the Enter Feed URL box. Tap Show Feeds... and a list of the available feeds will appear.

3.  If there's one you want to subscribe to, tap the + button beside it, and then the Add Feed button and select Done.

4. If there's not one that's right, search manually. Press View in Browser and you'll go to the site's home page. Here it's the New York Times. Scroll to the bottom and there's a link to RSS. Tap this and you'll see all the feeds available. Choose one and press Subscribe in the prompt box, and then click Done.

**Step 6**: From an RRS feed you can tap the Safari icon to open the article in your browser or tap the share icon to post it via Twitter or Facebook.

5. Tap Feeds and you will see all your feeds listed. Tap one, and a list of stories replaces the feeds in the side pane. Tap the story and the headline will appear in the main pane. Tap this headline, and a web page with the full article will be loaded.

6. Press the small compass icon and you can open the article in Safari, or tap the Share button and you can post the article to Twitter, Facebook or an online bookmark service to read later.

## Mix in Your Social Life

Described as a Social News Magazine, Flipboard allows you to mix in your news feeds from Google Reader, newspapers (such as the *Guardian* and *New York Times*), blogs and the like with information from your Facebook newsfeed, Twitter timeline, YouTube videos, Instagram photos and other social media.

As a result, you have a personalized magazine where your news and that of your friends, is scattered among national and international news, plus other feeds that match your interests.

## Hot Tip

A news feed – RSS feed – includes a summary of new articles, links, and details of when they were published. The feed is read by news reader software, which can pull in feeds from thousands of sources.

## Create Your Personalized Magazine

1. Go to the App Store and search for Flipboard. Press the Free button, and then Install App, and when it has finished downloading, tap to launch.

2. The front cover shows the main featured Flipboard stories, like any magazine, but unlike any printed issue, the stories change every few seconds.

3. Swipe the Flip button to the left to go to your main page. The tiles show different sources from which to create your personal Flipboard. Tap any tile to see more.

4. Once in a section, such as the *Guardian* newspaper here, tap the story to see the original article and pictures. Along the bottom are various icons for sharing the story – adding a comment, retweeting it, marking it as a favourite or posting it online to read it later.

**Step 4**: When you share a story on Flipboard you can choose to add a comment or tweet it.

5. Flip between the pages to see more stories and entries.

6. Tap the red bookmark with magnifying glass on it to see which sites and social networks currently make up your Flipboard. You can add more social networks from the list or search through the different categories that interest you to see more potential sources. You can also search by keyword.

7. When you find one you want to add to your board, tap the + button. If you create an account, you can also access your personal Flipboard from any device.

# MAGAZINES

**No more need to be weighed down with a pile of glossy magazines. Carry the contents of several magazine racks with ease on your iPad.**

## NEWSSTAND

Get the richness and vibrancy of your favourite magazines and newspapers, wherever you are, on the high-resolution iPad screen.

### Getting the Publications

Newsstand is a special folder that gathers together in one place all your magazine and newspaper subscriptions.

- **Newsstand:** Designed to look like the magazine display case you see in a library, Newsstand is built in to the iPad and can't be deleted or dragged into another folder.

**Above:** Newsstand stores and displays your newspaper and magazine subscriptions. Add publications to your collection by tapping the Store button, then the Newsstand tab.

- **Publications:** Each of the publications within Newsstand is a separate app, accessed from the App Store.

- **Empty Shelves:** When you first open Newsstand, it will be empty. To get your favourite publications, tap the Store button on the right, then the Newsstand tab. This links through to a section of the App Store.

- Tap the publication you are interested in to get the detailed information box, along with ratings and reviews from other subscribers.

- **Free**: Somewhat misleadingly, the price button is often marked as Free. This is because there is no charge for the app itself but there usually is to view the publication. Tap Free to download the app and the publication will be placed on a Newsstand shelf, then tap to open.

- **Individual**: As these are individual apps, they will each have their own look and feel. Typically, though, they'll show the available issues. Some may offer a preview edition or sample pages. However, most offer the choice of buying a single issue as an in-app purchase or a regular subscription, which auto-renews.

## Organizing Your Newsstand

Any purchases are made through your Apple ID account and if you subscribe, each new issue will be automatically downloaded over your Wi-Fi connection. A flash across the edge of the publication will highlight the fact that a new edition is available. A number in a red circle appears on the Newsstand icon on the Home page to show how many publications have new issues available.

## Rearranging Your Publications

The publication apps are placed in the Newsstand in the order you downloaded them. The newest ones appear top left. To reorder them, tap and hold a single publication until they all start to jiggle, then drag and drop them into their new location. Press the Home button to fix them in place. To delete a publication app, tap and hold until it starts jiggling and press the x mark in the corner.

## Turn Off Auto-renew for Subscriptions

When you subscribe to a magazine or newspaper, it is made clear that this will auto-renew. It puts the onus on you to remember to cancel your subscription if you no longer want it, before it's due for renewal. Although it's not made clear, you can cancel auto-renewal at any time.

**Above:** To reorder your publications, tap and hold one of them until they all begin to jiggle. You can then drag and drop them, or tap the cross to delete.

1.   Tap Settings, then iTunes & App Store (before iOS 6 it's just Store).

2.   Tap your Apple ID and in the box that opens select View Apple ID. You may be asked to enter your password.

3.   Scroll down and tap Manage App Subscriptions (if you don't have any, this button won't show). Choose the subscription from the page that opens and turn Auto-Renewal to Off, then tap turn Off in the confirmation box that opens.

# DIGITAL MAGAZINE VIEWER

Rather than reinvent a publication for the iPad, some publishers prefer to make the digital version as close to the original print copy as possible.

## Zinio

- **Digital editions**: With Zinio you get an exact copy of the print edition in digital format, plus, sometimes, extra content in the form of video and audio.

- **Digital publisher**: Claiming to be the world's largest newsstand, Zinio is the digital publisher for hundreds of magazines around the world.

- **Download the app**: You can then explore a series of free sample articles, which you can also share on Twitter, Facebook or LinkedIn.

- **Browse through different categories**: Browse to find the

**Above:** The Zinio app features exact copies of print magazine edition in digital format, as illustrated by this article from a film comment magazine.

magazines you want. They are usually available to purchase as a single issue or on subscription.

○ **Standard format**: The magazines are turned into a standard format, so they can be read through the Zinio reader, which is available for desktop computers, as well as for the iPad.

**Above:** Download the Comics app to buy and read comic books from major publishers.

## COMICS

With its great display and reputation as the Superhero of the Tablets, the iPad is a natural medium for reading comics and comic books.

### Comic Readers

○ **Many comic apps**: There are many apps to choose from that enable you to access some of the great classic comics – from the Beano to Marvel Comics and the X Men or DC Comics and Superman.

○ **Free to download**: Like newspapers and magazines, the apps are free to download but there are in-app charges for purchasing a single issue of a comic or a longer-term subscription.

○ **Comics**: Instead of downloading the apps separately, you can use apps like Comics, which are digital readers that let you buy and read comics and comic books from many of the major publishers. They publish many of the digital comics the same day as the print edition is published, so you don't miss out. You can search for titles according to popularity, genre, publisher and even creators. There are also free comics for you to try.

ENTERTAINMENT

# ENTERTAINMENT MACHINE

The iPad is as good a music player as any, with the advantage of a bigger screen to browse through your collection. But you'll need three apps – iTunes, Podcasts and Music – to get all the features you can access in iTunes on your computer.

## Hot Tip

To listen to your music, you can play it through the built-in speaker, attach headphones through the headphone jack, use wireless stereo headphones paired with your iPad via Bluetooth or play through your TV using AirPlay.

**Above:** The Music app appears by default as one of the apps in the Dock at the bottom of the Home Screen.

## USING THE MUSIC APP

This is the place to play all your audio content, whether it's music and audiobooks from iTunes, taken from your CDs or downloaded from the internet.

### Play Music

By default, Music is one of the main buttons in the Dock that's accessible at the bottom of every Home screen.

1. Tap the music icon to open it, then Songs and the name of the song you want to play.

2. In the music controls at the top of the screen, press the Play button (a right-pointing triangle) to start the song. While the song is playing, this changes to the Pause button (marked by two vertical lines). Press this at any time to pause the music and press again to restart.

3.  In the centre section the red line (playhead) moves to the right along the scrubber bar to show how far you are through the song. Tap and move the playhead backward and forward, and you can move to a different part of the song.

4.  You'll also see time counters at either side. On the left it shows how long the song has been playing. On the right it shows how much time remains before the song ends.

**Above:** The iPad music player displays the controls, scrubber bar and volume slider at the top.

5.  Above the progress bar you'll see the name of the song that's playing and the artist. To the left, tap the Repeat button (two arrows in a loop) to repeat all the songs in that playlist. Tap it twice to play the current song again. To the right, tap the Shuffle button (two arrowed lines meeting and separating) and the songs in the playlist will be played in a random order.

6.  On the far left, tap the Back button to go to the previous song or the Forward button to move to the next song. If the song is playing, tapping the Back button just returns to the start of the track.

7.  To alter the volume, use the slider at the top or the physical buttons at the side of the iPad.

## Album View

When a song is playing, tap the thumbnail of the album cover to show it in the Now Playing screen. Tap again to see the music controls. In this view, you can browse the songs just by swiping through the album covers. The music starts playing automatically.

**Above:** Tap a thumbnail to display your music in album view, swipe through the album covers to start playing songs automatically.

1.  Tap the Information button in the bottom-right corner and you'll see all the tracks from the album that you have in your collection.

2.  Tap the row of dots above the list to give your rating to songs. This is useful if you later want to create a smart playlist in iTunes, such as one that includes all your five-star rated music. Tap the button again to return to the previous window.

3.  When you're ready, tap the left-pointing arrow at the bottom to return to the song list.

**Hot Tip**
To display the music controls quickly when you're in another app, double-press the Home button and swipe to the right.

### Let Siri Be DJ
On the iPad 3 and later, take the stress out of changing track and let Siri control your music. Start by tapping-and-holding the Home button.

○ **Play music**: say 'play music' or 'play'; 'pause' or 'stop' to halt the music; 'next song' or 'previous song' to change track.

○ **Play a series of songs**: dictate 'Play album <name>', 'Play artist <name>' or 'Play playlist <name>' and all songs under that name are played.

○ **Shuffle current playlist**: by saying 'Shuffle' while it's playing.

○ **Get track information**: ask 'What's playing?' or 'Who sings this song?'

# FIND YOUR MOOD MUSIC
The music you feel like listening to at any particular time will change. To make it easier to find the sound that suits your mood, your library of songs is sorted into different lists.

## Browse Buttons

To find the different way your songs are organized, tap the buttons at the bottom of the screen. You can browse through your music sorted by playlist, song title, name of the artist or album.

To see other categories, tap More and there are further options to view your music organized by genre and composer.

**Above:** Use the browse buttons at the bottom of the screen to display music by category.

## Search Songs

Rather than scroll through one long list, you can locate a particular song by typing its name in the Search box in the bottom-right corner. You can also search by album title, artist name or composer.

# ADDING MUSIC

You can add music directly to your iPad through the iTunes app or sync music gathered from other sources (as long as it isn't copy protected), through your computer.

## iTunes App

Access the online music store to download music directly to your iPad.

1.  Tap the app to go online to the iTunes store and select Music at the bottom.

2.  If there's a particular genre you like – from Pop to Hip-Hop – select it using the buttons at the top of the screen. If the genre you want isn't visible, tap More to see others.

3.  Scroll down the page and you can see different selections, such as new albums, themed collections, what's hot and what the Apple staff are listening to. If you know what you want, use the Search box at the top.

4.  Once you have selected an album or song, tap to go through to the information page. This includes details of the artist, the release date and average rating by other iTunes users, plus the price button. Underneath is a listing of the track(s).

5.  Tap the song title to listen to a 90-second sample of the track.

6.  To buy an individual track, tap the price button to the right and then the Buy button. If it's the album on which the track features that you want to buy, tap the price button at the top of the page.

7.  If you have a big collection, you may end up trying to buy a track you have already purchased. If this was bought in the iTunes store, Download appears instead of the price, so you won't be charged again.

**Step 6**: Buy a track by tapping the price button to its right, and then the buy button. To buy the whole album, tap the price button at the top of the page.

8.  While the items are being downloaded, tap the More button and then Downloads to see their progress.

## Other Music Sources

- ▶ **Amazon MP3 Store**: Amazon's online music store was the first to offer song downloads that were not digitally rights managed – that is, DRM-free – so they could be played on virtually any music player. Today, they still have a huge selection and offer consistently low prices.

- ▶ **Subscription music sites**: such as eMusic.com, where you pay a monthly subscription which entitles you to a number of downloads that can be synced with iTunes to play on your iPad.

- **Your music collection**: add your favourite tracks from your CDs or downloaded MP3 files.

- **Musician sites**: like Bandcamp – which lets musicians sell their music (as downloads) direct to fans.

# PODCASTS

There are thousands of hours of podcasts – audio and video shows – on a stunning range of topics that covers virtually everything from self-help to hobbies. Time to tune in.

**Above:** The Bandcamp website enables musicians to sell their music downloads directly to fans.

## Finding Podcasts

Previously, finding and playing a podcast involved two apps. You would first search and select a show using the iTunes app and then play the podcast from the Music app. Now Apple's free Podcast app is all you need. When you open the app, it will show your library with any podcasts already downloaded.

1. To see all the available podcasts, tap the Store button in the bottom-left corner. Browse through the different categories: you can see what's New & Noteworthy or featured comedy and sports shows.

2. To select different categories, tap More and see what else is available. Use the buttons at the bottom to search for only Audio or Video podcasts or to view charts of the most popular podcasts.

## Hot Tip

When you install the new Podcast app, it removes the podcasts and controls from the Music app. This means it's not possible to create playlists that include podcasts. If that is important to you, don't install the podcasts app, or delete it if you already have.

3.  Tap any that interest you, and the information box gives you full details of the available episodes, how long they are, together with other users' ratings and reviews.

4.  Tap the downward-pointing arrow beside a single episode to download just that one.

5.  Press the Subscribe button, and the latest episode will be downloaded. You will also get future episodes downloaded automatically as they become available.

6.  Press the Library button and you'll see the newly downloaded podcast there. The number in the blue circle shows the number of episodes that have not yet been played.

## Browse the Popular Podcasts

1.  In Library view tap the Top Stations button at the bottom of the screen. This shows the most popular podcasts in different categories.

**Above:** Browse the Podcast store by category and tap any that interest you to find out more information and download.

## Hot Tip

By default, auto-downloads is switched off. Once your podcast is downloaded, you can turn this on. Tap the podcast in your library list view, select the gear icon and turn on the Auto-Download button. If it's not visible, it is because you're not subscribed. Turn on the Subscription button and it will appear.

2.  Swipe the 'dial' at the top, left or right, to change the category. To explore the category you are in, swipe up or down.

3.  Tap the podcast icon to see details about the individual episodes. Press the i button to get more information.

## Play Your Podcasts

In your Library you can view your podcasts as a series of tiles (icons) or in list view by selecting the relevant button at the top left. There are two ways to play your podcasts:

**Step 2:** Browse popular podcasts within a category by swiping up or down.

○ **Streaming:** tap any episode and it will start playing without being fully downloaded first. To do this, you need to be connected to Wi-Fi.

## Hot Tip

If you have existing podcasts transferred from Music, you might get a message asking if you would like to sync your podcasts between all your iDevices that use the same Apple ID. To do so, press the Sync button.

○ **Download:** tap the download button next to any individual episode of a podcast, so it is stored on your iPad and you can listen to it even when you don't have a Wi-Fi connection. Once it's downloaded in your Library, tap the podcast to start playing.

## Control Playback

When you begin playback, the podcast controls appear. They can also be accessed from the Library by pressing the Now Playing button in the top-right.

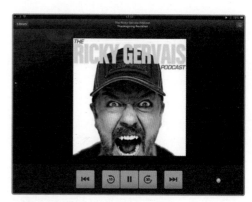

**Above:** Starting Podcast playback displays the podcast controls at the bottom of the screen.

## Audio Playback Controls

- **Backward button**: plays a previous episode.

- **Replay button**: with the number 10 inside a left-pointing loop: tap this to go back 10 seconds in the podcast.

- **Play/Pause button**: toggle this to start playing the podcast or pause it.

- **Skip Forward button**: with the number 30 inside a right-pointing loop – moves forward 30 seconds.

- **Forward button**: play the next episode.

- **Volume slider**: move left or right to set the volume.

## Additional Controls

More controls are hidden behind the podcast artwork. Swipe upwards and you'll see the outline of a tape recording deck with more buttons.

- **1x button**: lets you change the playback speed: 1x is normal, 1/2X plays at half speed, while 2x plays at double speed.

- **Playhead**: tap, hold and drag this to move to another part of the podcast.

- **Share button**: lets you send a link to the podcast by mail or text, or post as an update to Twitter and Facebook.

**Above**: Swiping upwards on the podcast artwork reveals additional controls such as the 1x button and the sleep timer.

○ **Sleep timer**: handy if you want to be lulled to sleep by music or someone reading a story. Choose how long you want the podcast to play before it stops.

## Video Playback Controls

There are similar buttons to control viewing of your video podcast. To access them, simply tap the screen while watching the video.

## Delete Podcasts

To remove podcast subscriptions, go to your Library. If the podcasts are in tiled view, tap the Edit button and then the x in the corner of the podcast you want to delete.

If you have the podcasts in list view, tap the Edit button, then tap the red icon beside the episode you want to remove and click the Delete button.

# SYNCING MUSIC

While the iPad is a great entertainment centre, it doesn't have as much space as your computer for holding all your songs, etc. So when it comes to syncing with iTunes, it pays to be selective.

## iTunes Sync

Connect the iPad to iTunes on your computer and it will appear in the top sidebar.

1. Click the Music tab at the top. The simplest option would be to check Sync Music and then Entire Music Library. However, as you are likely to have more music than will fit on your iPad, the safer option is Selected playlists, artists, albums and genres.

2. You can also choose to add music videos – although be careful if you have a lot, as these tend to be very large files and will quickly eat up your free space – and voice memos.

3. Now go through your playlists and select those you want on your iPad.

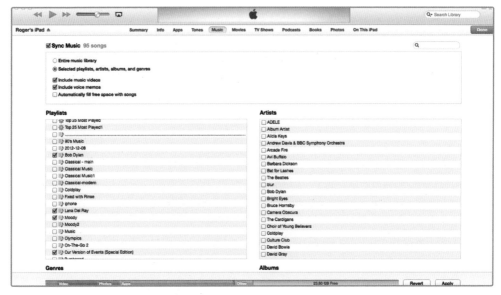

**Above:** When using iTunes to sync music from your laptop to your iPad, select the option to sync Selected playlists, artists, albums and genres. You can then go through these different categories and tick those which you would like to copy over to your iPad.

4.   Do the same for artists, albums and genres. Don't worry about duplication. Even if you choose an artist whose songs are on the playlists or genres you've also selected, only one copy of the actual song will be copied over – although you'll still see it referenced in each list.

5.   An alternative option is to create your own special playlist that has all the songs you want to copy over to your iPad. Then select only this playlist to sync.

6.   Click Apply to sync your changes now.

## iTunes Match

Subscribe to this service for an annual fee and you can sync your music collection using Apple's iCloud. All your music, including music from CDs or other online stores, will sync with Apple's servers rather than iTunes on your personal computer. You will see your entire music collection on your iPad but it will be stored on iCloud.

# ORGANIZING YOUR MUSIC

**The bigger your music collection the more difficult it is to keep under control. Fortunately, playlists make it easy to organize your sounds to suit your mood, while features like Home sharing and music streaming make it possible to listen to your music without overloading your iPad.**

## MUSIC SETTINGS

When it comes to playing your music, there are several features you can change to suit your personal preferences. Tap the Settings icon, then Music, to get started.

### Changing Sound Levels

○ **Sound Check:** turn this on to play all songs at roughly the same volume, even if an individual track is louder or softer.

○ **Equalization (EQ):** changes the quality of the sound to suit the type of music you are listening to. There are 23 different effects, ranging from Bass reducer to Spoken word. Generally, these settings apply only to music played through the Music app, except for Late Night. This setting applies to video as well. As it

**Above:** Choose from Equalization effects to adjust sound settings to suit certain types of music.

reduces volume in loud parts and increases it in quiet sections, it's particularly good for listening to music in a noisy place, such as on an aeroplane.

○ **Set a Volume Limit:** for when the children have grabbed the iPad to play their music. Tap Volume Limit, and then adjust the volume slider.

# PLAYLISTS

These are mini-collections – lists – of songs based on a theme, which can be as personal or as general as you wish. For example, you could have a playlist of the songs played at your wedding, all 1990s songs in your Library or your Adele collection.

## Create Playlists: Step-by-step

Playlists that you create on your iPad can be synced with iTunes on your PC or Mac.

1. Tap the Music app to open and then the Playlists button. There you'll see any existing playlists. To create one, tap the New button.

2. In the box that opens give the playlist a name that readily describes its content and tap Save.

3. The list of Songs on your iPad opens. Tap the + button beside those you want to add to the playlist or click the Add All Songs button.

4. Tap the buttons at the bottom to select songs by artist name, album title and so on, or use the Search box.

5. When you have added all the songs you want, tap the Done button.

6. Your new playlist will be copied to the iTunes library on your computer next time

**Step 2**: Enter a name for your new playlist and tap Save.

**Step 3**: Tap the + button beside songs you want to add to the playlist, or click the Add All Songs button.

you sync your iPad (or sync via iCloud if you
subscribe to iTunes Match).

## Edit Playlists

Rather than create a new playlist, you can change an
existing one.

1. Tap Playlists, select the playlist to modify and
   press the Edit button.

2. Tap Add songs to add more tracks to the playlist in
   exactly the same way as creating a playlist above.

3. To delete a song, tap the red button and then
   press the Delete button that appears on the right-
   hand side.

4. Tracks in the playlist are played in the order in which
   they appear. To change the song order, tap the Drag
   handle on the right and move it up or down.

5. To delete a playlist altogether, press the Playlists
   button, tap-and-hold the playlist then tap the X in
   the corner.

**Step 6:** Sync your iPad to copy your new playlist to
the iTunes library on your computer.

# Hot Tip

**Once you've set the volume
limit, stop someone else
changing it back. Tap Settings,
General, then Enable
Restrictions. Enter a four
figure Restrictions Passcode
and re-enter it for security.
Under Accounts, select
Volume Limit, and then tap
Don't Allow Changes.**

## Genius Playlists

Genius works two ways. In iTunes, the Genius Bar recommends music similar to the track that's
playing and that you can buy from the store. Alternatively, click the Genius button – the atom
icon – and you can generate a Genius playlist. Pick a song, and Genius will create a list of other
songs from your music collection that are related and go well together.

**Step 1:** Once you have turned on Genius in iTunes, sync iTunes with your iPad to start using it.

## Hot Tip

To add to the confusion, there are also Genius Mixes. These are a selection of songs in the same kind of music or genre. The mix is refreshed each time you play it.

**Step 6:** Genius-playlists are copied to your computer when you next sync your iPad.

## Creating a Genius Playlist

1. Before you use Genius on the iPad, turn on the feature in iTunes. Go to your Mac or PC, click Store in the Menu bar then Turn On Genius and click the button on the page. Enter your Apple ID and once Genius has got to work, sync iTunes with your iPad.

2 Play the song on your iPad for which you want related recommendations and tap the Genius button (with its atom icon).

3. The new Genius playlist appears in the list of playlists. Tap it to play the suggested songs.

4. If you're not keen on the recommendations, tap Refresh to get a new list.

5. Once you're happy with the playlist, tap Save and it will be named after the song title used initially.

6. Genius playlists are copied to your computer when you next sync your iPad. Once that is done, you can't delete it from your iPad. You will have to delete it or remove it from the sync list in iTunes on your computer.

## Deleting Songs

To delete a song from the iPad, press the Songs button, swipe the track you want to delete from right to left and press the Delete button that appears. This will remove the song from your iPad, but it will remain in your iTunes library on your Mac or PC, or on iCloud.

If you subscribe to iTunes Match, you can't delete the music tracks from your iPad. When you run short of space iTunes Match replaces the oldest, least played tracks with new music.

# HOME SHARING

Play music on your iPad from the iTunes library on your computer – without having to download the music files.

## Setting up Home Sharing

For Home Sharing to work, your iPad and computer must be on the same Wi-Fi network.

1.  Open iTunes on your Mac or PC, go to the File Menu, Home Sharing and choose Turn On Home Sharing.

**Above:** Select from the list to choose which libraries you want to share using Home Sharing.

2.  You'll be prompted for your Apple ID and password. Enter these and then click Create Home Share.

3.  On the iPad go to Settings, Music and under Home Sharing enter the same Apple ID and password.

4.  Open the Music app and select More, then Shared in the box that opens. You'll see the names of any libraries that are available.

5.  Tap one and you'll see the music from your shared library listed on the iPad. Select any track, and it will be streamed to your iPad from your computer.

# STREAMING MUSIC

Instead of storing and playing your own music, you can get songs, radio shows, concerts and more streamed, on demand, to your iPad.

## Streaming Music Apps

Don't be bound by the constraints of your existing music collection when you can take your pick from millions of songs and discover new artists through your own on-demand music service.

- Typically, these services offer the **wide spectrum** of music – from rock, pop and funk to the classics. Some include **talk radio**, covering sport and comedy.

- While several sites offer a free service with upgrade to **premium** paid features, such as removal of ads or listening offline, you usually have to pay a **monthly subscription** to get the most benefit from the iPad app.

- Among the services with iPad specific apps are **Spotify** (www.spotify.com), **Slacker Radio** (www.slacker.com) and **MOG** (www.mog.com). These last two are only currently available in the US.

**Above:** Spotify has an iPad specific app.

- Other on demand music services, such as **Last.fm** don't have a specific **iPad** app but do have **iPhone** versions that will run on your tablet.

- As Last.fm is a music recommendation service, the app **tracks** the music you and you friends have been playing and gives music **recommendations** based on that.

## Concerts

Get the best of the bands – from Coldplay to The Who – playing for you direct on your iPad. Qello streams HD concert film to your tablet. Subscribe and you get unlimited access to the concert vault and can design your own set lists.

## Airplay

For great sounds around the home, you can use Airplay to play music from your iPad through your Hi-Fi speakers, wherever they are.

All you need are AirPlay-enabled speakers, which are available from well-known manufacturers like Denon, B&W, JBL and so on in the Apple Store.

**Above:** Use Airplay to play music from your iPad through Airplay capable devices with Hi-Fi speakers, such as Apple TV.

As well as the music, all the information about it, such as the song title, artist's name, playing time and so on, are also streamed across your Wi-Fi network.

## Using AirPlay

1. To use AirPlay, tap your Music app to open. In the top-right corner you'll see the AirPlay symbol. Tap this to open the options box. You'll see the iPad and any other AirPlay-capable devices, such as Apple TV, on your home network.

2. Select the receiver you want to use and a tick appears beside it. In Music, tap a song and it will start to play through the device you selected.

3. Control the sound from your iPad, using Music's audio controls to play or pause a song, skip a track or change the volume.

4. To return playback to the iPad, tap the Airplay icon again and select iPad from the list.

## Stream to Your Computer

If you don't have AirPlay-enabled speakers, you can still get a bigger sound for your music (and see video on a bigger screen) by streaming it from your iPad to your Mac or PC. You will need some extra software to enable this iPad-to-computer streaming. AirServer (www.airserverapp.com) is inexpensive and available for both the Mac (used here) and PC.

**Above:** AirServer app allows iPad-to-computer streaming.

## Setting up Streaming

1. Download and install AirServer to your computer. You will need to activate it by entering your email address or activation code supplied when you purchased the software.

2. The AirPlay logo is now available in the computer's menu. Click and select Launch on Startup, so that the service is always running.

3. Select Preferences and Audio, and you can choose which speakers you want to use – typically, this will be System Default. Click AirPlay controls device volume to use the iPad as your remote control.

4. To connect your iPad to the computer, double-press the Home button and swipe to the right until you see the AirPlay button. Tap this and you'll see a list of AirPlay-enabled devices. Among them will be the computer on which you installed AirServer. Alternatively, tap to open the Music app and then select the AirPlay symbol.

5. In the options box select your computer, then tap your song and it will start playing through your Mac or PC.

6. To return to playing music on your iPad, tap the AirPlay button again and then select iPad.

# STORING MUSIC

**Despite the limited space on the iPad, it's possible to have access to your music any time, anywhere by using online storage services.**

## iTUNES MATCH

With iTunes Match you can access your entire music collection, even songs imported from CDs or bought online, from your iPad.

### Music Match-maker

iTunes Match is a paid subscription service that lets you store your music library in iCloud – that is on Apple's servers – rather than your own computer. It means you can access and play your music from your iPad virtually wherever you are.

### Getting Started

You have to sign up for iTunes Match on your computer. Open iTunes, go to File menu and select Turn on iTunes Match. Below the brief overview of iTunes Match click the button to subscribe and enter your details. Your subscription is tied to your Apple ID.

**Above:** Use iTunes to activate iTunes Match. You will be asked to enter your Apple ID.

### Matching Tracks

Once you're subscribed, iTunes Match looks through your music library, matching any tracks you have against the 26 million plus songs in the iTunes store. These are added to your music library in iCloud. The matched tracks play back at high quality – 256-KBps AAC DRM-free – regardless of the quality of your original track.

## Hot Tip

You can store up to 25,000 songs in iCloud (more if songs are bought from the iTunes store).

**Step 5**: Download tracks manually by tapping the iCloud symbol, which is shown here as it appears on iOS5/iPad1 models.

**Step 7**: For iOS 6 iPads, download a song stored on the iCloud by pressing the cloud icon shown here.

Any songs that can't be matched are uploaded to iCloud. How long this will take depends on the number of songs and the speed of your connection.

## Listen to Your Matched Music

1.  Go to Settings on the iPad, tap Music and turn on iTunes Match.

2.  Turn off Use Cellular Data, as streaming music files can quickly eat up your data allowance. Now you can stream or download a song only via Wi-Fi.

3.  iTunes Match will overwrite any existing music or playlists on your iPad, with full details of your iCloud library. In iOS 5 on iPad 1 a cloud symbol beside each track shows it is not on the iPad but is available online.

4.  Tap the song title and it will be streamed from iCloud, via your Wi-Fi connection, and downloaded fully as it plays.

5.  You can also download tracks manually, so you can play them when you don't have an internet connection by tapping the cloud button.

6.  Once you play a track on a playlist, playback continues automatically down the list, whether the song is already downloaded or is still in iCloud.

7.  With iOS 6 on later iPads this has changed. There are no icons showing whether tracks are online or stored locally. When you play a song stored on iCloud, it is streamed and not automatically downloaded. To download songs press the cloud icon on the playlist and all files will be downloaded.

8.  When you've ripped more music from CDs or bought more albums from online stores other than iTunes, you'll want to make sure your iCloud list is up to date. In iTunes on your computer select Store then Update iTunes Match.

> **Hot Tip**
>
> If you don't want to stream music from iCloud, you can make sure you're only playing tracks that are already downloaded to your iPad by going to Settings, Music and turn off Show All Music.

## iTunes Match vs iTunes in iCloud

iTunes Matching is a paid-for song-matching and storage service. iTunes in iCloud is a free service which means that anything you've bought from the iTunes store, such as music, can be automatically downloaded to your iPad.

**Above:** You can download the Amazon Cloud Player for iPhone onto your iPad.

## Other Cloud Services

There are several other online services that will let you store and play your music – either streaming it from the cloud or downloading to play on your iPad. Amazon Cloud Player lets you store songs bought from the Amazon MP3 store free of charge and you can upload your own music from your computer to the cloud drive for a small annual fee. Although there is no dedicated app for the iPad, the iPhone version works fine. Google Play has a similar Music service and store but there is no specific mobile app for iDevices.

# MAKE YOUR OWN MUSIC

Several popstars, including Justin Bieber and Adele, have been discovered after recording their songs at home and posting them online. Try for yourself, using the iPad to make your own music.

## TUNE UP YOUR LIFE

Whether you are a professional musician or have no musical knowledge at all, GarageBand for iPad will get you hitting the right notes.

### GarageBand

Apple's GarageBand is a fantastically sophisticated program, which lets you record backing tracks for your songs, videos or just your amusement. There are three types of instruments used to record sounds.

- **Smart instruments:** great if you have no musical know-how. They cover guitars, keyboards, bass and drums and ensure all the notes and chords you play are in tune with each other.

**Above:** You can use GarageBand's touch keyboard to play and record songs.

- **Touch instruments:** best if you play guitar, bass, keyboards or drums for real. Tap the virtual instruments on screen to create your sound, but beware: they are pressure sensitive. The harder you press, the greater the volume of the piano note or sound of the drum.

- **Real instruments:** give the most authentic sound. You'll need to connect your guitar, keyboard or drum pads to the iPad directly. For example, you can connect a USB keyboard to the USB port using Apple's Camera Connection Kit.

# RECORD YOUR SONG

GarageBand for the iPad is a paid-for app available from the App Store. Download and install, then tap to open.

1. Choose your instrument. Swipe left or right to see what's available. In this example, the keyboard is selected.

2. The keyboard opens. Tap the image of the Grand Piano and select the type of keyboard, from Electric Piano to Heavy Metal Organ.

3. If you don't like the keyboard layout, press the keyboard button on the right and you have two rows of keys for left and right hands.

4. Tap the keys to play your notes. The spot where you tap and the force of your tap dictate the precise sound and volume.

**Step 2**: Tap the Grand Piano image and select a keyboard type, such as Electric Piano.

5. Tap the button in the middle to change how the keyboard moves when you swipe it. Glissando is more like a piano, whereas swiping plays the notes smoothly. Switch to scroll and swiping moves you left or right on the keyboard.

6. When you're ready to record, tap the red Record button in the top bar. The metronome starts and counts through one measure before recording begins and the Play button turns blue. Tap this to stop recording.

7. If you fluff the notes, tap the Undo button and start again. Press the View button to change to Tracks view, where you can see the music you recorded. Tap once to select it and press the Play button to listen to it.

**Step 8:** Tap the loop icon and drag a clip from the list onto the mixing deck.

8. To add to your song, tap the loop icon and drag a pre-recorded clip from the list onto the mixing deck. Tap Instruments and select other sounds to record, like drum, guitar or bass.

9. To save your song, tap My Songs in the control bar.

## Build a Song

To create a song in GarageBand, you record the Touch instruments and then arrange the recordings in Tracks view. You can have up to eight tracks.

1. Select Tracks view in the top control bar. You'll see each row is a track, which has the recording of one Touch instrument, shown as a rectangular block. The icon beside the recording shows which instrument it is.

2. Swipe this icon to the right to reveal the track controls where you can control the relative volume of the track within the song.

3. Move blocks of music around by tapping-and-dragging them to new positions in the song. To trim the clip, push the edges in.

### Hot Tip
Double-tap on a track – or region as it's called – and you get the editing controls: Cut, Copy, Delete, Loop and Split.

## Sharing a Song

Once you're happy with your song, there are several ways to share it. Tap My Songs, then the Edit button. Select the one you want, and then tap the Share button in the top-left.

You'll see there are options to share the song on social media, such as Facebook or YouTube, add it to iMovie to use in your own videos, email it or save it as a ringtone.

# GAMES

When it comes gameplay, the iPad's large screen gives it a natural advantage over its smaller screen rivals, particularly if you have a Retina display to display the high-quality graphics.

## STANDALONE GAMES

Whether you're a casual or serious gamer there's plenty to keep you entertained with apps specially made to take advantage of the iPad's increasing processing power.

### Games Store

Download games direct to the iPad from the App Store. Simply tap the App Store icon to open and select Games from the top bar. In the box that opens you can select All Games categories or choose the one that interests you most. As you will see, there are games that cover the whole spectrum from action and adventure to board games, racing, strategy and puzzles.

### Popular Games

There are thousands of games available in the App Store, so it's good to get personal recommendations. To see what others are playing, select the App Store, tap the Games button on the top menu and then Top Charts at the bottom.

Hot Tip

Playing with touchscreen controls takes a little getting used to compared with physical controllers, so it might be as well to practise before challenging friends.

**Above**: Download games from the App Store by selecting Games in the top bar, browse by looking at All Games or choosing a category.

Here you can see the most popular free and paid-for games, as well as those that have grossed the most money. If there's a particular type of game you're looking for, such as Arcade or Kids, tap the All Categories button in the top-left, select Games and make your choice.

Below are five of the most addictive games that also show why the iPad is great for gaming.

○ **Angry Birds Star Wars**: who wouldn't be angry when you're blasted through space. Amazingly popular and compulsive to play, Angry Birds are now the rebels having to battle Darth Vader in a Star Wars adventure. If you get tired with that fantasy, don't forget there's Angry Birds Space, Rio, Seasons and so on.

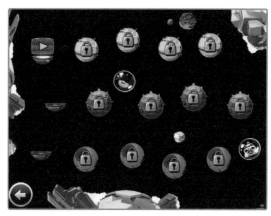

○ **The Dark Knight Rises**: most blockbuster films now have a tie-in game to build on their popularity. This one gives you the chance to be Batman and fight your way, with the help of some useful gadgets, through the dark streets of Gotham City.

**Above**: Angry Birds is one of the most popular games in the App Store. There are many different versions to try.

○ **Tiger Woods PGA Tour**: experience life as a golf pro, stand on some of the world's best fairways, check out your swing and see how you stack up against the real pros. You can also earn rewards by completing challenges across other golf games.

○ **Scrabble**: the traditional word game has had a makeover and comes with exclusive features for the iPad. There are HD Graphics to take advantage of the iPad screen, sound effects and animations plus up-to-date dictionaries to help put a stop to the arguments about what words are allowed.

○ **We Rule Deluxe for iPad**: Create your own kingdom with what is described as the longest-running social game for iDevices. With elements of that other mega popular game Farmville, you not only harvest crops but you can expand your territory to include shops, roads, rivers and even world landmarks like Buckingham Palace. The social element is that you can add celebrity friends or your own friends from real life, roam their kingdoms, buy from their shops and so on.

# SOCIAL GAMING NETWORK

Test your gaming skills against your friends – or strangers around the world – using Apple's multiplayer gaming app, Game Center.

## Getting Started with Game Center

Game Center works on the premise that gaming is more fun when done socially. Game Center itself is a built-in app that lets you play games against other people,

**Above**: The Game Center app lets you play games against other people and shows leaderboards of scores.

see what apps are available and get some bragging rights (or not) by showing a leaderboard of best scores on a game.

1. Open the Game Center app by tapping its icon, and then enter your Apple ID and password to sign in. If you want a separate Apple ID for gaming, tap Create New Account instead.

2. Even if you are signed in through your existing Apple ID, you can change the details that show in the Game Center.

4.  Tap the banner with your Account ID and choose View Account. Scroll down to your Nickname and you can enter a new one. Under Email, tap Add Another Email... to include any other email addresses you may have, so it's easier for your friends to find you.

5.  Under Privacy, tap to switch off Public Profile if you want only your friends to see your profile and don't want to be recommended to play with other gamers you don't know. If you are happy for everyone to see your details, turn this on. Tap Done when finished.

## Playing a Game

Tap the Games button at the bottom of the screen. You can go with any of the recommendations there or, to buy a particular game you want, tap the Find Game Center Games banner.

Here you'll see all the free and paid-for games for the iPad, sorted into different categories, that have been developed to run in Game Center. Tap the one you're interested in and press the price (or Free) button and then Install App Download.

Once it's downloaded, tap the Game's icon and you'll see the game's leaderboard. Tap the Play Game banner. Depending on the game, you can access the Game Center by tapping the Game Center icon on screen or pressing the Home button and then selecting Game Center from the Home screen.

**Above:** You can choose a game from the suggested recommendations or tap Find Game Center to search for a specific game.

## Playing with Friends

1. When you're ready to try out your skills against some competition, tap Friends, choose one, select the game and tap Play.

2. If no friends are listed, send a request. Tap Friends or Requests on the bottom bar and enter their email address or Game Center nickname in the address bar. To add them from your Contacts list, tap the + button.

3. If more than two players can play the game together, select additional players to invite and tap Next. Send your invitation and wait for the reply.

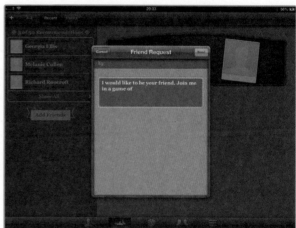

4. If none comes, or your friend isn't available, tap AutoMatch and Game Center will find someone to play. Alternatively, you can tap Invite Friend to try someone else you know.

**Above:** To play games against friends, send out requests by tapping Friends or Requests and entering their email address. You can also add friends from your contacts by tapping +.

5. Once everyone is ready, you can start the game.

6. If a friend invites you to play a paid-for game you haven't got, you will have to purchase it. To do so, tap Friends, then their name. Tap the game you want, then tap the price at the top of the screen.

### Hot Tip
Once you have achieved some impressive scores, you can challenge people to try to beat you. Tap the score or achievement you are proud of and then tap Challenge Friends.

# LIFESTYLE

Whether it's an essential life skill, such as cooking, or life enhancing, such as a Vogue Cropped T-Shirt, it will be covered in one of the thousands of lifestyle apps available for the iPad.

## SHOPPING

The high street has gone online. Most major retailers have an online store accessible using Safari on the iPad. Many have also developed their own tablet apps, from department stores such as Debenhams to fashion stores (H&M), home furnishing (Ikea) and food delivery services such as Ocado. That's not forgetting the original online retailers Amazon and eBay, which are still prime destinations for iPad shoppers.

There's also a new breed of online store, such as Fancy, with dedicated apps for the iPad. Fancy is part social network, shopping catalogue and wish list. Ideas are crowd-sourced, recommended by savvy users, but unlike other collector sites such as Pinterest, the majority of items are also for sale.

**Above:** The Fancy iPad app allows you to share your wish lists and purchases with other users.

## FOOD AND DRINK

Foodies in need of a recipe can try Epicurious, which also creates shopping lists based on the dish you choose. If you can cook only with expert advice from celebrity chefs, try Gordon Ramsey Cook with Me HD or Jamie's Recipes from Jamie Oliver. To wash it all down, mix your own Speakeasy Cocktails.

# SPORTS

The sporting life is covered, with everything from the Everyday Golf Coach HD, analysing your swing, to ESPN ScoreCenter for iPad, covering results and news from sports around the world.

# HEALTH AND FITNESS

Got a spare moment? Do some exercise with Fitness HD or Pocket Yoga HD. Go too far and you may need a medical self-help app to aid the diagnosis, but it must be remembered that an app should never replace medical advice from a health professional.

# TRAVEL

Wherever you're planning your trip, there's an app to help. TripAdvisor lets you check out hotels, flights and restaurants in your planned destination with reviews and ratings by other users. If you prefer to travel in spirit rather than the flesh, fly around the planet from your iPad with Google Earth, explore different cultures and distant lands with the digital app version of National Geographic Magazine or explore the universe with NASA App HD.

**Above:** There are many weather apps which can be adjusted to your location.

# REFERENCE

Previously, when there was a lively discussion in the pub or elsewhere, it was difficult, if not impossible, to prove who was right. Now it takes a moment's research on the iPad. What causes a plane's vapour trail? Look it up in Wikipedia, through one of the companion apps like Wikipanion. Get the low-down on the high-life of Al Capone in Encyclopaedia Britannica or test your romantic streak with a look at the sonnets in the app that covers the complete works of Shakespeare. More mundanely, what are the prospects of rain for the school sports day? Check it out with one of the myriad of weather apps that can be customized to your locale.

WORKING

# NOTES

One of the key ways of staying organized is to jot down a note when something occurs to you. With the Notes app you can sync with other iDevices and your computer, so you're always on top of what you have to do.

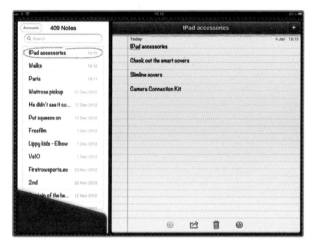

**Above:** When viewing notes in portrait mode the note that is currently open is circled in red in the left-hand pane.

## Hot Tip

If you don't like the font used for writing notes, tap Settings, then Notes and select a different one.

## TAKE NOTES

Notes isn't designed for writing your novel or essay, as it doesn't have the rich formatting features of programs such as Word, but is perfect for writing notes.

### Add a Note

Tap the Notes icon of a yellow ruled writing pad on your Home screen. Notes will automatically open the last note that you wrote. If this is the first time you've used Notes, you can just tap the screen where you want to type, and the keyboard appears. To start a new note, tap the + button in the top-right corner.

### Navigating Notes

It is easy to navigate your notes.

1.  In portrait mode, tap the Notes button and a pop-up window lists all your Notes accounts.

2.  Tap All Notes, and they are listed with the date they were written or updated, from the most recent to the oldest.

3.  The note that's currently open is circled in red. Simply tap the note you want, and it opens in the main window.

4.  To search the text of your Notes, tap the Search box and type in the word or phrase you are looking for.

5.  When the iPad is in landscape mode, the list of accounts and notes is permanently shown.

6.  In Notes view you can also move between notes by pressing the left-facing arrow button to go to the next note or right-facing arrow button to go to the previous one.

### Delete Notes

Tap the dustbin icon at the bottom of the screen to remove a note. In list view swipe left or right across the note title and then tap the Delete button.

## Hot Tip

The title of your note is the first line of text, which means you can end up with some pretty odd headings. It's a good idea to put the title you want as the first line of text.

# SYNCING NOTES

So you can always be up-to-date with your jottings, you can sync notes between your iPad, your PC and other iDevices, as well as share them directly with others.

### Sync with iCloud

Use iCloud to keep any notes made in the Notes app on the iPad in sync with your computer and other devices, such as the iPhone and iPod Touch.

If you're using an Apple email address with iCloud (such as yourname@me.com or yourname@mac.com), tap Settings then iCloud and switch Notes to On.

**Above:** If you have an Apple email address you can sync your Notes through iCloud by toggling Notes to On in the iCloud settings menu.

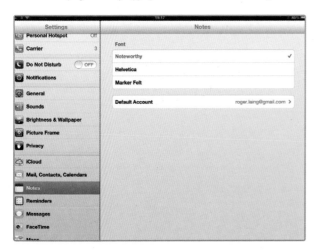

**Above:** When you create a note it will be attached to an email address. You can change this default address through Settings.

Alternatively, if you're using Gmail or a similar email account with iCloud, then go to Settings, select Mail, Contacts, Calendars and turn on Notes for the account.

## Share Notes

While reading the note, tap the Share button at the bottom of the screen. You can then choose to email the note, send it as a message or print it, using AirPrint.

## Notes Accounts

When you create a note, it is attached to a specific account. You can have several different accounts in Notes.

- **Email accounts:** as well as an account for notes created On My iPad, there may be others. Typically, these are attached to email accounts. In many email readers you may see a notes folder that contain these messages. There is usually an option to display the notes or not.

- **Different accounts:** all of these can be accessed in Notes itself, by tapping the Accounts button (in portrait mode you may have to tap the Notes button first).

- ○ **Specific accounts**: to see only the notes in a specific account, choose that account from the list. If you then tap the + button, it will create a new note in that account.

- ○ **Default**: to choose which account to use as the default for new notes, go to Settings, tap Notes and make your choice.

# TAKE ACTION

Notes doesn't just list what you have to do, it also helps you get started. That's because it's smart enough to recognize the different types of text in your message.

## Follow the Links

When you see text that is underlined, tap and hold the link. A pop-up menu appears with the available options.

- ○ **Phone numbers**: select and you can Add to Contacts. Tap again and you have the further option to add this to an existing contact or create a new one.

- ○ **Street address**: select Open in Maps to see the location and get directions or Add to Contacts.

- ○ **Date**: select this and then press Create Event. In the box that opens you can enter details of what's happening, the location, start and end time and the

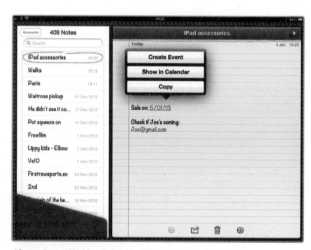

**Above:** Tap and hold underlined text to view options. Tapping on a date allows you to create an event or view it in your calendar.

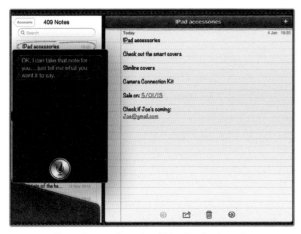

**Above:** Summon Siri, request 'Take a Note' and start dictating.

calendar to add it to. Alternatively, select Show in Calendar and it will open your Calendar app, so you can see if you're free that day and what else may be happening.

- **Email address**: press and you can choose to start a new message to that address, add it to your Contacts or copy it to the clipboard to use in another app.

- **Web address**: press the link, and it opens the page in Safari.

# DICTATE YOUR NOTES

As a virtual personal assistant, Siri is just what you need when it comes to finding, dictating and updating your notes. Unfortunately, he only works with an iPad 3 or later.

## Find a Note

Summon Siri by tapping-and-holding the Home button. Ask to 'Show all my notes' or notes with the keyword you are looking for, such as 'Show my note about birthday presents.' Tap the note in Siri's list and it opens in the Notes app.

## Dictate Your Note

Get right to the point and tell Siri to 'Take a note' and then dictate your message.

## Update a Note

If it's some time since you wrote the original note you'll first have to find it. Tell Siri, 'Update Note' and select the one you want from the list. Alternatively, give sufficient detail to help Siri find it, such as 'Update note on February sales forecasts' and then dictate the additional text. Tap on the microphone when finished.

# DOCUMENTS

The iPad lets you create, view and edit documents just as if you were at your desktop computer, and has built-in sharing and syncing too.

## CREATE DOCS

While a touch screen keyboard may not be as practical as the one on your computer for creating long or complex documents, it is still possible to produce some great-looking work.

### Writing on iPad

Given that it is a mobile app, Pages is an amazingly powerful word processor. It is a paid-for app, so you will first have to buy and download the program from the App Store.

### Creating a Document

1. Tap Pages to open it. The first time it's launched, the Welcome screen offers different options, such as using iCloud to store Pages documents.

2. On the Documents screen tap the + button in the top-left corner. If you already have documents created in Pages on your Mac or elsewhere, there are options to connect via iTunes or a web browser and download them. If you are starting from scratch, tap Create a Document.

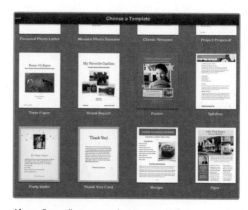

**Above:** Pages allows you to choose a template from existing formats, or create your own by selecting the Blank option.

3. Choose a Template from the selection, which includes pre-formatted documents, such as posters, party invites, plus different letter and report styles. To create your own, select Blank.

4.  When you open a template, it will include dummy text. To edit this and replace it with your own, double-tap the screen, and the keyboard will appear.

**Above:** When editing a document you can change the preset template text by highlighting the passage you want to change. Use the keyboard to enter your own text and the options in the top bar to adjust settings such as font size and alignment.

## Editing a Document

○ **Change the text**: highlight the part you want to alter and use the settings in the rule bar to change the font, font size, alignment and so on.

○ **Edit styles**: for paragraphs and headings, etc. select the text and tap the Paintbrush icon in the top bar. Tap the Layout tab and you can change the number of Columns and Line Spacing.

○ **Add Photos, Tables, Charts or Shapes**: just tap the + button in the top-right and make your choice.

○ **Resize a graphic**: tap it and push one of the blue anchor points to amend.

○ **Settings**: press the spanner in the top-right corner and Document Setup to alter paper size, margins and so on.

## Working with iWork

Pages is part of the iWork suite of programs, which also includes Numbers for spreadsheets and Keynote for presentations. The iPad apps don't have all the features of the Mac versions of the programs. So when you import a Pages document from your Mac to iPad, you may see a warning notice.

If you have iCloud set up on your iPad, the three iWork apps will automatically back up their documents to Apple's servers. The changes are then synced to your Mac and iDevices, so any alterations made to your documents on the go are immediately available when you're back in the office.

## Sharing iWork Files

While iCloud makes it simple to move your iWork documents between your Mac or PC and different iDevices, there are other ways to share your files.

## Sharing Documents

When the document is open in Pages, Numbers or Keynote, tap the tools button – with the spanner icon – at the top, then select Share and Print.

- ○ **Email**: sends the document as an email attachment, in the format you choose. This can be as an iWork, PDF or Microsoft Office file.

- ○ **Print**: sends the document to any available network AirPrint printers.

**Above**: Share your documents by selecting from the options in the Share and Print menu.

- ○ **Open in Another App**: first select the format to save it in, then choose from the list of available apps that can open it.

- ○ **Copy to iTunes**: to add it to the file sharing section where you can transfer it to your PC or Mac.

- ○ **Copy to WebDAV**: lets you use your browser to transfer the files to a network server via the web.

## Dealing with Numbers

Numbers for iPad lets you create and edit your spreadsheets on the go. Even if you're sent a spreadsheet that wasn't created with Numbers, you can work on it, as the program can open Excel documents or spreadsheets saved as comma-separated value (.csv) files.

## Getting Started with Numbers

Open Numbers and you have a choice of templates, from expense reports to a loan comparison, savings sheet or invoice. To set up your own, select Blank. Choose one to get started and tap to open.

> **Hot Tip**
>
> Although there is no PC version of the iWork suite, the files can be saved and transferred in a format that can be used by Office-compatible programs or viewed as PDFs.

- ◯ **Edit text**: to change the text in a cell, double-tap, then tap to select the text entry box that appears and type in your changes. The Text icon (T) on the keyboard should also be selected.

**Above:** Numbers provides you with a variety of template options to use as the basis for your document by entering your own data and words.

- ◯ **Edit numbers**: double-tap the cell where you want to change the figures and select the Numbers icon (42) to open the calculator.

- ◯ **Equations**: for more complicated spreadsheets. Tap the = icon on the keyboard and you have access to a calculator with a wide range of functions, from the financial to the statistical.

- ◯ **Date and time**: can be added by selecting the clock icon from the keyboard, accessed by double-tapping a cell.

## Change Styles

To alter the appearance of your spreadsheet, tap a cell and then press the paintbrush icon on the top bar. Choose the relevant tab to alter:

- **Table Styles**: select the Table tab and choose the layout you prefer or set them manually by tapping Table Options.

- **Headers**: extend the size of header rows and columns and add a footer if required.

- **Cells**: tap Text Options to change the font, size and colour. Use the other buttons to alter alignment and the Border Style or the Fill Colour of the cell.

- **Format**: you can change the cell format so that, instead of a number, it contains a percentage, date, text or checkbox, etc.

## Creating Presentations

Could business life survive without the presentation? Certainly not at the moment, so if a presentation is needed quickly or there are some last minute changes to your slides, Keynote on the iPad is your answer.

- **Start a New Presentation**: open Keynote and tap the + symbol in the top-left and then Create Presentation. To get started, choose one of the stylish templates available as your theme for the slides.

- **Edit the Presentation**: the theme is a single page at the moment. To add more, tap the + icon in the bottom-left. To edit the current slide, just double-tap on the text and type in your changes using the keyboard that appears or press the microphone and dictate to Siri (iPad 3 and later).

**Above:** Cell text options allows you to adjust font characteristics and styles so that any headings or labels appear as you would like them to.

## Hot Tip

The easiest way to see changes in your data is to add a chart. Tap the + button on the Numbers toolbar, select the Charts tab and choose the type of chart to add. Tap the blue box to select the cells on which the chart is based.

- **Change Styles**: tap the paintbrush icon and you can change font sizes and styles, the appearance of lists and the layout.

- **Resizing Images**: double-tap the picture and use the blue anchor points to adjust the size. Tap the paintbrush icon on the toolbar and you can style the borders and flip the image.

- **Build Your Presentation**: press the spanner icon and you can change the way the slides build up and the transitions between them. You can also add Presenter Notes, share and print your presentation.

**Above:** When using Keynote for presentations you can change styles by tapping the paintbrush icon and selecting from the options displayed.

## Blogging on iPad

Often the best ideas for your blog come as you browse the web. Blogsy for iPad takes advantage of this by having its own built-in browser, which makes it easy to drag-and-drop images and web links right into your blog post.

Likewise, you can add photos and videos from your iPad or photo albums on sites such as Facebook and Flickr with just a swipe of the finger. As it supports most blogging platforms, including Wordpress, Blogger, Tumblr and TypePad, it should work well with your personal and professional blogs.

## Drawing on iPad

Celebrated British artist David Hockney pays testament to the brilliance of the iPad as a drawing tool. He has used the Brushes app to create more than 400 works, first on the iPhone and then on the iPad. Several of the works were displayed, on the iPad, naturally, at the

**Above:** You can use the iPad as a very effective drawing tool, as demonstrated by the successful series of works produced by David Hockney using the brushes app.

exhibition Me Draw on iPad in Denmark's Louisiana Museum of Modern Art.

# EDIT DOCS

As many businesses use Microsoft Office for their word processing, spreadsheets and presentations, there are apps that let you work with these on your iPad.

## Office on the Move

Documents To Go® is an all-in-one application for managing your business documents. It lets you view, create and edit Microsoft Word (word processor) documents, Excel spreadsheets and, if you upgrade to the premium edition, PowerPoint presentations. In addition, the paid-for version works with your Apple iWork files, Google Docs and other online file storage services, so you have all your business files together in one place.

## Getting Your Office Files

A desktop version of Documents To Go for both Mac and PC provides two-way syncing with the iPad, so any changes you make to the files are automatically updated. You can also open documents sent as email attachments.

## Google Docs

Rather than keep your files on one computer, online storage services let you access your files and in some cases edit them from anywhere you have internet access. Among the most popular services for business is Google Docs. With this free service, the documents you create are stored on Google Drive.

**Above:** Use the Google Drive app to access and organize documents stored on Google Drive.

1.  Use the Google Drive app, available from the App Store, to access your documents.

2.  Click the Edit Document button to do some basic editing.

3.  Choose Who Has Access to create a virtual workspace where you can invite colleagues to view reports, presentations and so on. You can choose whether to let them view, comment or edit the documents.

## Hot Tip

If the file sharing section isn't visible it means that you don't have an app that can share files through iTunes. It will appear once you do.

## SYNC DOCS

While some apps let you sync your business documents with iCloud and other online storage services, the majority use iTunes to transfer files between your PC or Mac and the iPad.

### File Sharing

1.  Open iTunes on your computer and click the iPad icon on the top menu bar, then Apps.

2.  Scroll down the page to the File Sharing section and choose the app from the list on the left that has the files you want to transfer.

3.  On the right it will show all the documents on the iPad. Select one and click the Save To button to select where to save the file on the computer.

4.  To transfer a file from your computer, click the Add button and browse to where it is located then click Open.

# PRINT DOCUMENTS

While we increasingly view documents on a screen of some size, there are times when we do need to print out a hard copy.

## AirPrint

AirPrint is Apple technology that's built into the iPad's operating system, so you can print directly to a printer. Unfortunately, it's not quite that simple. The printer itself has to be AirPrint-enabled and on the same wireless network as your iPad.

## Hot Tip

There's a growing list of manufacturers, available on Apple's website, who have added AirPrint support to their printers.

## Print through Your Computer

With this method you install a program on your Mac or PC that receives your print job from the iPad and sends it to the printers your computer uses. Among the programs available are FingerPrint (www.collobos.com – Mac and PC) or Printopia (www.ecamm.com/mac/printopia – Mac only).

## Print Wirelessly

Provided the printer is on the same wireless network as the iPad, there are apps that will print directly to Wi-Fi printers. If your printer is physically connected to your computer, by the USB port, for example, several apps have a desktop helper application for your computer, so you can wirelessly send your document to your Mac or PC to process for printing. Apps available include PrintCentral and Printer Pro.

**Above:** You can install the Fingerprint program on your Mac or PC and use it as a means of wirelessly printing your iPad documents.

# CALENDAR

**The hectic pace of modern life makes it more important than ever to get organized. With your iPad digital assistant you can keep up-to-date with all your calendars – at work and play.**

## MANAGE YOUR SCHEDULE

The Calendar is a core app that's already on your iPad. Use it to set up your events and set alerts, so you don't miss anything.

### Calendar Views

Select the view you want – by day, week, month, year or list – by tapping the tabs at the top. Each calendar uses a different colour to mark its events, so you can see at a glance when there are busy work periods, for example.

### Creating Events

1. In any view, tap the + button, and a new event box appears.

2. Enter a name and location for the event.

3. Tap the Starts section to bring up the date and time controls, and enter the details.

4. Select Repeat and choose how frequently it reoccurs, then select the calendar to add it to. When finished, tap Done.

**Above:** Tap the + button to add a new event to your calendar by entering the name, location, time and details.

## Use Siri

Even if you're not in the Calendar app, you can get Siri to add an event or check what you've got coming up if you have iPad 3 or later.

1.  Press and hold the Home button, and when Siri responds, give the event details, e.g. 'Schedule haircut 3pm next Tuesday.'

> **Hot Tip**
>
> In all but the year view, you can also tap-and-hold until the new event box appears and then release to open the Add Event box.

2.  Siri will check to see if there's a conflicting event. If there is, he will give the details and ask if you want to proceed.

3.  To see what's coming up, ask Siri: 'What appointments do I have today?' or 'What's happening on Thursday?'

## Edit Events

Tap the event and then tap the Edit button. In week or month view, if you've got the wrong day, just drag the event to a new date.

## Search Events

If you know there's something you've been invited to but can't remember the date, search events. Tap List from the top menu bar and then enter the keywords you're looking for – such as Jeff's presentation – in the Search box.

## Setting Alerts

Adding an event to your calendar is one thing, but many of us need a reminder when it's about to happen. Alerts are set in the Add Event box.

1.  Tap the Alert button and select how long before the event you want to be reminded. The options vary from a couple of weeks before to the actual time of the event.

2. For events such as birthdays, you probably want an earlier alert, so you have time to get a card or present. You can set the default alert period in Settings, Mail, Contacts, Calendars. Scroll down to the Calendars section and select Default Alert Times. You can change these for timed events, birthdays and all day events.

**Above:** You can set specific timed alerts for different events.

# SHARING CALENDARS

In one calendar you can view lots of different calendars at once, including web-based calendars or even Facebook events and birthdays. You can also choose to share individual calendars with others.

## Subscribing to Calendars

1. If you use an online calendar, such as Google or Yahoo!, add this by going to Settings, Mail, Contacts, Calendars, and then tapping Add Account. Select from the list or tap Other if your calendar service isn't named.

**Above:** You can add Facebook events and birthdays to your calendar by toggling Calendar to On in Facebook settings.

2. To add Facebook events, tap Settings, Facebook and under Allow These Apps to Use Your Account turn on Calendar (not available on iPad 1).

3. To select which calendars to view, open the Calendar app and tap the Calendars button. You'll see they are separated in the different accounts. Tap those you want visible.

## Sharing Events

1.  The calendar system is linked to your email. On certain email systems, such as iCloud or Microsoft Exchange, you can send and reply to meeting invitations.

2.  To invite others, tap an event, and then the Edit button. Tap Invitees and select them from your Contacts by clicking the blue + symbol.

3.  To reply to an invitation, tap the Invitations button at the top of the screen or tap the invitation in the calendar. You can see who's organizing it and who else is invited. If you add comments, only the organizer will see them.

## Sharing iCloud Calendars

Instead of individual events, you can share complete calendars you have on iCloud, such as for a work project, with others. They will need an iCloud account.

Tap the Calendars button and in the section under the email address used for your iCloud account select the calendar you want to share. Under Shared with: tap Add Person and tap the + button to choose from Contacts. An invitation is emailed to them to join the calendar.

**Hot Tip**

Your colleagues will need an Apple ID and iCloud account to accept your invitation to share a calendar.

## Make Your iCloud Calendar Public

You can make your iCloud calendar viewable by anyone, although they can't change anything. Follow the steps above and turn on Public Calendar. Tap Share Link and email or text the URL to anyone you want to view a read-only version of the calendar.

**Above:** You can share your iCloud calendar by adding contacts to the Shared with box, and make it public by toggling Public Calendar to On.

## Sharing Other Calendars

If you want to keep a wider group, such as the office football team, organized and be sure they all know what's happening, use your iPad to set up and share a calendar on one of the free services, such as Google.

1.  Download and install the Google Search app, then sign in to your account, if you have one, or create a new one. Rather than share your personal calendar, set up a new one. Tap Calendar, then change to Desktop view. When the calendar loads, tap the arrow beside My Calendars and select Create new calendar.

2.  Fill in the details. Enter the email addresses of those you want to use it in the Share with specific people section and then tap Create Calendar.

## Hot Tip

Making your project calendar on iCloud public is a good way of sharing important milestones with a project team.

**Above:** Use your Google account to create a new calendar and select who you want to share it with.

3.  Now set up the Calendar app on the iPad. If you don't already subscribe to a Google calendar, tap Settings, then Mail, Contacts, Calendars and select Gmail. Fill in your account details and tap Save.

4.  Open the Calendar app, tap the Calendars button and under your Gmail address you'll see the new calendar has a tick beside it. Now enter events, making sure that the name of the shared calendar is the one used in the Add Events box. Now those sharing your calendar will also see the event.

# SYNC CALENDARS

There are several ways to make sure your calendars stay in sync but once you have chosen one, stick with it, or you'll end up seeing double.

## iTunes

You can sync your calendar on the iPad with a similar app on your computer, such as Microsoft Outlook or Apple iCal, using iTunes.

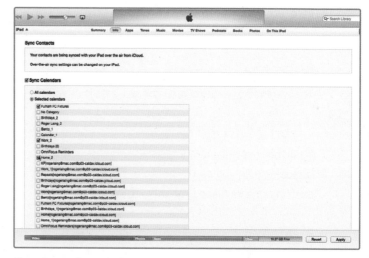

1. Connect the iPad to your Mac or PC and click iPad on the top menu bar and then the Info tab. Click the Sync Calendars with box and select the type of calendar from the drop-down list.

**Above:** You can choose whether to sync all or some of your calendars via iTunes by clicking the relevant boxes in the drop-down list.

2. You can choose to sync all calendars or just those you select. To save space and time, you can also choose not to sync events older than a certain period of time, such as 30 days.

## iCloud

By syncing via iCloud, any events you add to your calendars on your computer or iOS device can be updated on all of them, so you don't have to keep re-entering information.

1. Tap Settings, then iCloud on your iPad and turn on the button beside Calendars.

2. Go to Calendar, then tap the Calendars button and select which of the calendars listed under the Apple ID email address used for iCloud you want to sync with.

# CONTACTS

**Your Contacts app is far more than just a list of names and addresses; it is also your social hub from which you can send an email, text or even Tweet.**

## MANAGE CONTACTS

There are many ways to keep contact details of your friends, family and colleagues up-to-date.

### Import Contacts

If you have your list of contacts elsewhere – in Gmail, webmail or an email program such as Outlook – then you don't want to re-enter them one-by-one. Fortunately, you can import your contacts to iCloud and sync them to your iPad.

1.  As iCloud is built into the iPad, all you need to do is to activate it, using your Apple ID. Go to Settings, then iCloud, and make sure Contacts is turned on.

2.  On your Mac or PC go to your existing mail program or webmail account and export all contacts in a single vCard file. How this is done will vary but the program's help file should explain what to do.

3.  Still on your computer, access iCloud in your browser by going to www.icloud.com. Sign in with your Apple ID and password, then select Contacts. Click the Settings button with its gear icon that's in the bottom-left and click Import vCard.

**Above:** Once you have turned Contacts on in your iCloud settings the app will appear in your iCloud home screen.

4. Browse to where you saved the vCard and select it. This will import the contacts online, which will then be synced to your Contacts address book on the iPad.

## Sync Contacts by iTunes

As an alternative to using iCloud, you can sync your contacts using iTunes.

1. Connect your iPad to iTunes and select it from the top menu bar, then press the Info tab.

2. Select Sync contacts and you have the choice of keeping all of them up-to-date or tapping Selected groups and checking the box beside those to sync.

3. The first time you sync with the iPad, you'll be asked if you want to merge the data, replace the contacts list on the iPad or replace the contacts on your computer with the information on the iPad.

4. You can sync contacts data from the Address Book, Microsoft Entourage or Microsoft Outlook on the Mac or Windows and others.

**Above:** Manually add contacts to your iPad by filling in the various details within each Add Field box and tapping Done.

## Add Contacts Manually

In order to add a contact directly to the iPad, tap the Contacts app to open it, then press the + button. A blank form appears. Enter the details, tapping the return key on the keyboard to move between fields.

Tap the green button beside add field, and there are options to add a contact's nickname, the phonetic pronunciation of their name, birthday, Twitter handle and so on. Tap Done when finished.

## Find/Locate Contacts

As your popularity grows, so will your address book, which makes it difficult to find the contact you're looking for. Here is what to do to navigate through your contacts quickly.

- **Search**: tap the Search field and use the keyboard to start typing the name. Notice that only those names that contain the letter will appear. As you type more letters, the list narrows.

- **Tap the initial letter of the contact**: from the tabbed list on the left of the page to jump to that point in your contacts book.

- **Ask Siri**: for example, say, 'Find Thomas Smith' or if you have established your relationship with some of your contacts, ask: 'Find Mum,' for example.

**Hot Tip**

Don't worry about formatting, such as putting capital letters at the start of someone's name or dashes in phone numbers, as Contacts handles these automatically.

**Above**: Search your iPad contacts by tapping search and beginning to type the name you are looking for until it appears in the list below.

## Set up Relationships for Siri in Contacts

On iPad 3 and later, Siri can use Contacts to send text messages or emails, but it is much easier if it knows who are the key people in your life.

- **Tell Siri who you are**: Siri needs to know who he's talking to. Go to Settings, General, Siri and tap My Info. Select your contact details from the pop-up window.

- **Add your relationships**: Whether it's your boss, girlfriend, mum or big brother, let Siri know the link to individual contacts by saying, for example: 'Vicky Alexandra is my daughter.' Siri will ask you to confirm the information.

○ **Dealing with a large family**: It could be confusing if you have several daughters, so you may have to be more specific about the relationship, such as oldest daughter or youngest daughter.

## Add Relationships Manually

Tap the Contacts app to open it, select your name and then the Edit button. Tap on add field, then Related people and a relationship field is added to the page. Tap the label name and change this to the right relationship, such as brother, sister, friend, and then tap the name field and select the contact from the list. Tap Done when finished.

# USING CONTACTS

Once you have family, friends and colleagues set up it's easy to get in touch with them, direct from the Contacts app.

## Sending a Message through Siri

When you have let Siri know who your key contacts are, you can simply speak your message. For example, tell Siri: 'Text my boss I'm running late for the meeting.'

Siri will locate the contact and ask you to confirm the message. If it's correct, tell Siri to 'Send.' Say, 'Change it' to alter the message or 'Cancel' to abandon it.

**Above:** Add relationships manually by adding a relationship field to the page and then entering the correct relationship and adding their contact details.

**Hot Tip**
If the right label to describe your relationship is not listed, create it yourself. Scroll down the list of label names, tap Add Custom Label and enter the name you want.

## Off the Page

- ○ **Save to memory**: tap-and-hold a name or phone number, and it will be copied to memory, so it's easy to add to an email or message

- ○ **Send an email**: tap an email address, and it opens a new email with the address already filled in. Just add a subject line and your message.

- ○ **Share contact**: this opens a new message with all the information about the contact saved as a vCard. If you have saved any personal information with this contact, it will also be included.

- ○ **Send a message**: select the number to use to send a text message.

- ○ **FaceTime**: this button shows only if you have FaceTime activated. To do this, go to Settings, FaceTime and turn it on. Tap the button, and it starts a video call.

- ○ **Add to Favourites**: this is linked to FaceTime and adds the contact to your FaceTime favourites list.

**Above:** You can share your contacts by sending an automatically compiled vCard by email or text.

# SOCIAL MEDIA CONTACTS

On iPad 1 Twitter, and on later iPads Twitter and Facebook are built-in apps. The result is that you can add friends' Twitter handles and usernames as well as other details to their entries in Contacts.

## Add Twitter

There's nothing to stop you adding Twitter details when you enter a contact's details but there is a much quicker and more certain method.

1. Go to Settings and tap Twitter. Assuming you have set up your account (*see* page 79), tap the Update Contacts button. This will compare email addresses and phone numbers from your Contacts with those used in Twitter.

2. Any matches, and Twitter usernames and profile photos will be added to individual contact details. You'll see the progress bar while it's happening, and then the number of contacts updated.

3. Tap Contacts and you'll see that several will include a Twitter username and the avatar – or profile picture – they use.

## Tweet from Your Contacts

Tap your contact's Twitter username. Select Tweet and it opens a Tweet box that's already addressed to them, so you can just enter your message and press Send. Alternatively, select View Tweets and you're taken to a Twitter page showing all their latest posts.

## Add Facebook

Facebook works in a similar way to Twitter above. It also adds a profile photo and marks it with a small Facebook logo.

Facebook has its own messaging service and will try to use this as the default email address, rather than the one used to sign up for the service. It adds this Facebook address to the contact's details.

## Hot Tip

Any contacts using iOS 6 will see your Facebook email address as your preferred option. To check, go to your Facebook timeline, tap the About link and go to the Contact info section. If it's the @facebook address that's listed, tap the Edit button and change it to the address you want to use.

**Above:** Tap on a contact's Twitter username to send them a tweet or view their tweets.

# REMINDERS

**While you can use Notes to create your to-do lists, Reminders goes a step further. Not only does it let you list your tasks and check them off, it also provides a timely alert when you have something to do.**

## SET UP REMINDERS

Reminders help you to organize daily life by setting up a list of all you have to do. As with Calendar events, you can set these up with dates and alarms when they have to be done or simply list them with no prompt.

### Setting up Reminders – Step-by-step

1. Tap the Reminders app, which is now built in to the iPad operating system, and then tap the + sign in the top-right corner.

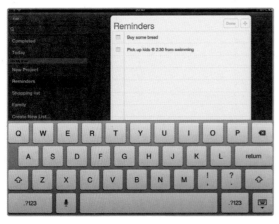

**Step 2:** After opening the Reminders app, add new reminders by tapping the + sign. Use the virtual keyboard to type your list, separating each by tapping the return key.

2. Using the virtual keyboard that appears, type in your item 'to do', such as buy some bread or pick up kids from swimming and then tap the Return key. The titles don't need to be long, just descriptive enough to remind you what has to be done. To edit them, just tap again.

3. Add more details if you want. Tap Show More, and you can add Notes. You can also choose the priority – from high to none – as well as choose which list to add it to.

4.  That's where you could leave it. Many to-do apps offer simple checklists that rely on regularly checking what to do next. Reminders goes further and will let you know when something needs doing. Tap the reminder in the list, then turn on Remind Me On a Day.

5.  Tap on the date and time and use the dials to specify when you want the reminder, and then tap Done.

**Step 3:** You can prioritize your reminders by selecting options from High to None.

## Create New Reminder Lists

When you create a reminder, it is added to the list in Reminders. For easier organization you can create your own 'to do' lists with more meaningful names, such as Family, Work projects and so on.

Tap Create new list in the panel on the left and then write in the name using the on-screen keyboard.

## Repeat Reminders

Once you have set a reminder, you can repeat the alert, which can be handy if it's something that has

**Step 5:** To set alerts for your reminders you can choose a date and time using the dials.

to be done in stages, such as someone's birthday, where you have to be reminded in time to get a card and post it, and then call them on the day and so on.

## Search Reminders

Enter keywords in the Search box in the top-left, and a list of any completed and outstanding 'to-dos' appears. Tap one to select it. Use the mini-calendar in the left-hand panel to look for all reminders due on a certain date.

# DICTATE REMINDERS

If typing your to-do list is just another task you'd rather do without, get Siri to fill it in for you if you have an iPad 3 or later.

**Above:** You can use the mini calendar grid to quickly and easily view which reminders are due on which date.

## Timely Reminders

Tap-and-hold the Home button to access Siri and then say what you want to be reminded about – and when. For example, 'Remind me to book the restaurant for 7.30pm.' Before you say or tap Confirm, you can change the details by saying, 'Change the time to 8pm' or say, 'Cancel' to delete the event.

## Choose Your List

The reminder will be added to your default list, which is typically Reminders. To change the default, tap Settings, then Reminders and Default List. You can also tell Siri where to add your reminder. For example: 'Add butter to shopping list' or 'Add book DJ to party list.'

**Hot Tip**

Through iCloud you can sync Reminders, so they'll appear on your other iOS devices, such as iPhone or iPod Touch, as well as on a Mac computer running the Mountain Lion operating system. Go to Settings then iCloud and turn on Reminders.

**Above:** You can use Siri to remind you of items on your to do list, and help with other tasks such as recording your shopping list as you dictate it aloud.

**Above:** To delete reminders swipe right to left and tap Delete.

## COMPLETED TASKS

When a task is done, there's a tremendous sense of satisfaction from being able to mark it off as completed. Although it's finished, you can still review it. However, when your lists start to get too crowded, you'll want to remove tasks for good by deleting them.

### Complete Reminders

Select a list or date from the left to view your reminders. To mark a task as completed, tap the checkbox beside it. Tap Completed, and you'll see, in date order, all the tasks you've finished.

### Delete Reminders

Select the to-do list, or Completed view and you can delete individual items by swiping across the entry from right to left and tapping the Delete button.

Alternatively, tap the reminder you want to delete, and in the Details window that appears tap Delete, or Cancel if you change your mind.

### Hot Tip

If you have created a new reminder list you no longer need, tap the top-left Edit button, tap the red button beside the name of the list to remove and then press the Delete button. When you remove a list, it also deletes any remaining reminders.

ADVANCED iPAD

# CUSTOMIZING YOUR iPAD

Make the iPad your own by modifying the background and changing the ways different apps and controls work.

**Step 1:** Select Brightness & Wallpaper from the Settings menu to display icons previewing the current wallpaper.

**Step 2:** Tap the icons to select a new wallpaper image from the pre-supplied options or your own photo albums.

## PERSONALIZING THE EXPERIENCE

Keep the pictures that mean the most to you – family, friends or landscapes – as your background, associate different sounds to individual events and set up your iPad to work the way you do.

### Changing Wallpaper – Step-by-step

The wallpaper for your iPad is pasted to your Home screen and on the Lock screen.

1. In order to change it, tap Settings and then Brightness & Wallpaper. The large icons under Wallpaper preview the current wallpaper.

2. Tap this and select Wallpaper to choose a different, Apple-supplied image, as here, or access one of your own photos from the albums below.

3. Select the image you want and see it full view. If it's one of your own photos, you can adjust it to fit the screen. Tap and drag the image to centre on the part of the photo you want as your background.

You can also pinch to enlarge or reduce the size of the photo.

4.  Tap Set Lock Screen to use it as the wallpaper there or Set Home Screen if you want it to be the background for that screen. Set both will use the same image as wallpaper on both screens.

## Sounds

Make your iPad operate as noisily or quietly as you wish by turning on or off the sounds that go with different events, such as tapping on the keyboard.

1.  Tap Settings and then Sounds. At the top is the slider that controls the volume on incoming FaceTime calls. When Change with Buttons is turned on, the slider also controls the Alert volume. When turned off, the volume for each is set separately.

2.  Go through the list, and you can change the sound that plays with individual events; for example, the tone you hear each time you get a new voicemail, send a Tweet or trigger a Reminder Alert.

3.  Turn the Lock Sounds on, and a sound plays when the Lock screen is unlocked. Similarly, switch Keyboard Clicks on if you want to hear a click each time you tap a key on the on-screen keyboard or off if you prefer not to.

**Step 4**: To set an image as your Lock Screen background tap the Set Lock Screen option.

**Above**: Adjust options in the Sound Settings list to customize which sounds your iPad makes.

## Hot Tip

Rather than stick with the limited choice of Alert Tones supplied as part of the operating system, you can create your own.

## Create Your Own Sounds Using iTunes

There are various apps for creating your own ringtones, which can then be synced with your iPad using iTunes. You can also create great sounds from your music collection, using iTunes on your computer. Here the ringtone's created on a PC.

1. First choose the song you want to use from your iTunes library. Right-click, select Get Info then Options.

2. In the Start time, enter the time point from where you want the ringtone to start playing. (If you're not sure where this should be, play the song in iTunes and note the time for the start point from the main bar at the top).

3. In the Stop Time add 30 seconds to the Start Time and click the OK button. Right-click the song and select Create AAC version (once this is done, go back and uncheck the Start and Stop time, so the full version of the song plays in future)

4. Select the short version of the song in iTunes, right-click and select Show in Finder. Highlight the song title, change the file format at the end from .m4a to .m4r and confirm this in the dialogue box that opens.

**Above:** When setting your own ringtone from your iTunes library enter time points in the Start Time and Stop Time boxes and tap OK to choose which part of the song you will hear.

## Date and Time

If you're travelling, it's easy to change the time and date to match your planned destination. Go to Settings, General, then select Date & Time.

- **24-Hour Time**: turn this on if that's your preference and the iPad will display that time format (13:12 instead of 01:12 PM) in the status bar at the top of the screen.

- **Set Automatically**: turn on and the iPad will get the correct time based on your Wi-Fi or mobile connection. If you're still on your way to your final destination, you won't want this. Turn this setting off and the Set Date &Time field appears, so you can make your changes manually.

- **Time Zone**: tap this and in the Search box type the first letters of the nearest city. Select it from the list underneath, and it will automatically enter the time and date for that location.

- **Set Date and Time**: lets you adjust the settings manually. Tap the Date and then roll the controls underneath to the correct settings. Tap Time and do the same and then tap the Set Date & Time button to return to the main screen.

## Modifying the Keyboard

The more you use the iPad, the more you'll come to rely on the on-screen keyboard. Fortunately, you can get it to adapt to your way of working and add your own short cuts. Go to Settings, General and then press Keyboard.

## Hot Tip

Get the time around the world with the built-in Clock app. Tap to open and select the World Clock tab. Tap any clock face to open the Search box for a city in the time zone you want. A white clock face shows it's daytime, a dark face night-time.

- **Auto-Capitalization**: automatically capitalizes those pesky first letters of a sentence or name that you may forget to do.

- **Auto-Correction**: the faster you tap, the more likely you are to make mistakes. This will automatically correct common errors.

- ○ **Check Spelling**: always handy when you're writing an email to the boss.

- ○ **Enable Caps Lock**: by default this is turned off. When it's turned on, you can • double tap the Shift key to activate it, so that everything you write is in capital letters.

- ○ **"."**: looks strange but is very useful. By double-tapping the space bar you can automatically add a full stop and a space at the end of any sentence.

## Changing Keyboards

Tap the Keyboards button to change the layout to match your language or country, whether it's for Canadian English or traditional handwritten Chinese. To swap between Keyboards, tap the Globe icon on the bottom row of keys of the on-screen keyboard.

## Split Keyboard

Turn on if you want to separate the keyboard to different sides of the screen.

### Hot Tip

One of the easiest ways to divide the keyboard is to tap-and-hold the keyboard key on the on-screen keyboard, and then slide your finger to Split. To return to a single keyboard, press the same key and select Dock and Merge.

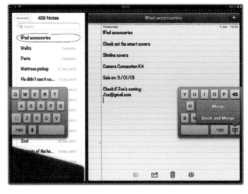

**Above:** Split and merge your keyboard by tapping the keyboard icon and selecting Split (left) and return to single keyboard by tapping the icon and selecting Dock and Merge (right).

## Short Cuts

These can potentially save a lot of time if there are several common phrases you use in Word documents or emails. There's one already written. Type omw and it's automatically written out in full as On my way! To add your own, such as a tagline to add to all your emails, tap Add New Shortcut... write out the full phrase and then add the letters you want to use as a short cut.

# SUSPENDING NOTIFICATIONS

Do Not Disturb will silence alerts and FaceTime calls for a period of time that you set. A moon icon is shown in the status bar at the top of the screen when it's active.

## Turn on Do Not Disturb

This is a new feature in iOS 6 (so is not available on the iPad 1). It prevents notifications from lighting up your screen or making a sound – but only when your iPad is locked or sleeping. To turn it on, go to Settings, then Do Not Disturb and press the On switch beside it.

## Change Your Do Not Disturb settings

Go to Notifications and tap Do Not Disturb.

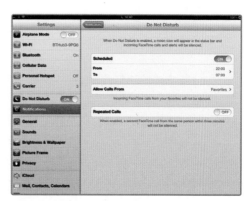

○ **Scheduled**: lets you select the quiet hours, the automatic time period when Do Not Disturb operates. For example, this could be at night from 22:00 to 07:00 when you're likely to be sleeping.

○ **Allow Calls From**: this creates the exceptions to the Do Not Disturb rule and allows incoming FaceTime calls from your Favourites or selected Contacts.

**Above:** Customize your Do Not Disturb settings via the Settings menu.

○ **Repeated Calls**: if someone's calling you urgently, they can get through. By turning this on, the second call will ring through if the same person calls twice within three minutes.

# iPAD'S OPERATING SYSTEM (iOS)

iOS is Apple's operating system for mobile devices such as the iPad, iPhone, iPod touch and, just to be different, Apple TV. iOS is regularly updated with new features.

## Updating to a New Version

Each new version of iOS fixes some problems, such as security patches for Safari, as well as adding new features. Because some of these additions, such as Siri, depend on a lot of processing power they are not available on all versions of the iPad. For example, you can only upgrade the first generation iPad to run iOS 5 (currently version 5.1.1), whereas the iPad 2, 3, 4 and mini can all be upgraded to run iOS 6 (currently version 6.0.2).

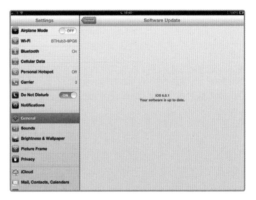

**Above:** If there is an update available it will be ready for wireless download and installation from the Software Update area.

Even so, there are some physical differences that mean that not all features in iOS 6 are available on each model – for example, Siri can't run on iPad 2.

## Updating Wirelessly

Tap Settings, General, then Software update. This shows the version number and if an update is available. If there is a newer version, follow the on-screen instructions to download and install the update. If your battery is less than half-strength, you'll be warned to connect your iPad to a power source.

## Updating via iTunes

Connect your iPad to your Mac or PC and click on your iPad's name in the top menu bar, then the Summary tab. You can see the version and a message stating when iTunes will next automatically check for an update. If you don't want to wait until then, click the Check for Update button. If one is available, follow the instructions to download and install.

# BROWSER SETTINGS

While you control the way you browse the web through Safari itself, some of the default settings, such as your search engine of choice, are changed elsewhere.

## Changing Safari

Go to Settings and tap Safari in the list on the left-hand side.

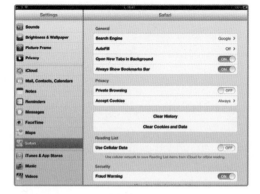

**Above:** Select Safari from the Settings menu to alter your internet browsing settings, such as turning on AutoFill and adjusting how new tabs are opened.

○ **Search engine:** Google is the first choice of most, but you can change this to Yahoo! or Bing.

○ **AutoFill:** repeatedly filling in the same information on web forms is a nuisance. Turn AutoFill on and it will use your info from the Contacts app or other forms you've previously completed. If you turn on Names and Passwords, Safari will remember the username and passwords used to access some websites.

○ **Open New Tabs in Background:** turn this on and when you tap for a new page, it appears in the background while you stay on the page you have open.

○ **Always Show Bookmarks Bar:** turn this off, and the bookmarks bar appears only when you have saved bookmarks.

# GENERAL SETTINGS

Select General from the list of settings, then About. Tap Name and enter a new one for your iPad. This is used when you connect to iTunes or sync your apps with the computer.

You can also see the Capacity of your iPad, while Available shows how much space you have left. This section also lists how many songs, videos, photos and apps you have stored.

## App Settings

Most apps downloaded from the App Store have settings that you can change to customize the way they work. Typically, these are applied within the app itself. There are other, more general settings, which apply to an app, that are controlled through the iPad's Settings app.

**Above:** Select General from the Settings menu to enter a name for your iPad and view its remaining space capacity.

1.  Tap the Settings app on the Home screen. On the left, underneath the list of built-in apps, are the other apps that have additional settings.

2.  Tap them to see what's available. Some of them have very little information – for example, the BBC iPlayer simply gives a version number.

3.  Others offer a much more extensive range of settings to change. With Hootsuite, for example, you can change font size, the number of messages to load as well as where to save photos.

4.  Once you have changed a setting, tap the button at the top to return to the previous screen.

## Hot Tip

Even though your iPad is described as 16GB, 32GB or 64GB, the Capacity shown is always less. For example, a 64GB shows as 57.2GB. The difference is taken up by the operating system and other files that make your iPad work.

# TROUBLESHOOTING

**While most problems on the iPad are easily resolved, there are times when you'll have to dig a little deeper to get the best performance and keep it running smoothly.**

## CONNECTIVITY

For most people Wi-Fi is the main way they connect the iPad to their home network. When it goes wrong, there are a series of steps to take to try to sort the problem.

### Wireless

Check initially that the problems aren't with your Wi-Fi network. The easiest way is to see if other devices are able to connect and working properly. If they're not, restarting your router might sort out the glitch. If the problem is just on the iPad, try the following.

○ **Turning on Airplane mode:** tap Settings then switch the button beside Airplane Mode to On. After a few seconds turn it Off. This will force the iPad to quit the network and try to reconnect.

○ **Restarting Wi-Fi:** tap Settings, then Wi-Fi, select the network you were connected to and tap the Renew Lease button.

○ **Re-entering the network settings:** follow the same path as the restart but this time tap Forget this Network. Then hard reset the iPad by holding down the Home button and Wake/Sleep button

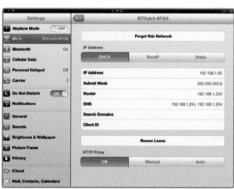

**Above:** Restart your Wi-Fi by tapping Renew Lease or Forget this Network and then resetting the iPad.

together until the iPad restarts and the Apple icon appears. Tap Settings, Wi-Fi and re-enter your network settings.

○ **Resetting the network**: Go to Settings, tap General, then Reset and press the Reset Network Settings button.

# SYNC PROBLEMS

Given the complexity of the task, there are surprisingly few problems with syncing your iPad – and those there are can be quickly resolved.

### Syncing New Apps

Great: you've bought the latest version of a killer game or fantastic app from iTunes, but it isn't syncing with the iPad. What to do?

○ **Make sure you're running the latest version of iOS**: some apps can run only on the most advanced version of the operating system. To see if an upgrade is available, go to Settings, General, then Software Update.

○ **Look to see if you have enough space**: particularly if there's an error message in iTunes

**Above:** If an app isn't syncing properly it may be a space issue, use iTunes to check how much space is left on your iPad.

or the app isn't fully downloaded during a Wi-Fi sync (the app's icon will appear dimmed on the screen and the progress bar will be blank).

○ **Make space for new apps:** apps are compressed for downloading and then expanded during installation, so even if you have space to download the app, there may not be room for the full app. Back up your iPad, then try deleting similarly sized apps and try again.

> ## Hot Tip
> TV shows and movies will probably take up the most space on your iPad. Rather than download them, stream them from your computer to your iPad using Home Sharing.

## Ghost Apps

These sometimes appear when syncing goes wrong – especially over Wi-Fi. The app's icon will appear on screen dimmed, but when you try and launch the app, nothing happens.

○ **Delete the app on your iPad:** tap-and-hold the icon until all apps start to jiggle, then press the delete button.

○ **Delete the app in iTunes:** if the above doesn't work, connect your iPad to your computer, select it in iTunes and click on the Apps tab. Scroll to the Home screen where the app is and delete it, then click Apply to sync with your iPad.

○ **Do a hard reset:** press the Home button and Wake/Sleep button on the top together and keep holding them until the Apple logo appears on the iPad to show it has restarted.

## Sync Problems with iTunes

Syncing by Wi-Fi or cable with iTunes is very convenient, until you find that your iPad appears to have vanished.

○ **Syncing by Wi-Fi**: it may be a simple problem of the network having crashed momentarily. Switch Wi-Fi off and on on the iPad by going to Settings and toggling Airplane Mode on then off. You may also have to relaunch the Wi-Fi connection on your Mac or PC.

○ **Restarts**: first try closing and then re-opening iTunes on your Mac or PC. If this doesn't work, restart your iPad and Mac or PC.

**Above:** If your internet crashes, you can toggle Airplane Mode on then off in your Wi-Fi settings to reconnect it quickly.

○ **Syncing by cable**: also check you are using the right cable (the iPhone charger cable is very similar but doesn't carry the same power) and try a different USB port to see if that makes any difference.

## Sync Problems with iCloud

Although we are used to everything happening quickly, details you enter in your calendar or new bookmarks aren't synchronized instantly. You should only worry that there's a problem if nothing is syncing.

○ **Are you on the same network?**: make sure that you are using the same Wi-Fi network and account details for iCloud on your Mac and iPad. If necessary, try deleting and re-entering the information.

○ **Make sure that sharing is enabled**: on the iPad go to Settings, iCloud, then Account. You should also check that the various services – Mail, Contacts, Calendar, etc. – are turned on and set to sync.

# iPAD BEHAVING BADLY

Sometimes, even the very best things go wrong: when the iPad freezes, apps crash or are not performing, try these steps, which are progressively more severe, to resolve the issue.

- **Quit the app**: if it refuses to do as you want, try closing the app. Double-press the Home button to open the multitasking bar, then swipe across the bar until you reach the icon for the app. Tap-and-hold this until the icons start shaking. Tap the red circle with the white minus sign to remove the app.

- **Force the App to Shut Down**: if the app refuses to leave quietly, you'll have to make it. To force quit hold the Sleep/Wake button at the top for a few seconds until the Power-Off slider appears. Now hold the Home button for about the same time – 10 seconds – and you'll be back on the main Home screen, but the app that was open will have closed.

- **Restart iPad**: as with many an electrical device, simply turning the iPad off and then on again can do wonders. Hold down the Sleep/Wake button at the top and when the Power-Off slider appears, slide it across to shut down the iPad. Press the Sleep/Wake button again to restart the iPad.

- **Reset iPad**: this clears most problems. Press-and-hold the Home button at the same time as the Sleep/Wake button at the top and continue to do so until the iPad restarts and the Apple icon appears.

**Above:** If an app crashes find it on the multitasking bar. Tap and hold until it starts jiggling and tap the red circle to quit the app and remove from the bar.

**Above:** Restore your iPad by connecting it to iTunes and selecting Restore iPad from the Summary tab.

◎ **Restore iPad**: whatever has gone wrong, now you can try to get round it by rolling back to the most recent backup you have for the iPad. Connect the iPad to your Mac or PC, select it from the top menu bar in iTunes and then press the Summary tab. Click Restore iPad. Select the most recent backup to restore your software and settings.

◎ **Recovery mode**: if Restore fails to complete, the iPad stops responding or continually restarts but never reaches the Home screen, then this is the ultimate step.

1. Connect the USB cable to your computer's USB port but don't yet attach it to the iPad.

2. Turn off the iPad the normal way. If it doesn't turn off, press and hold the Home button and Sleep/Wake button until it does.

3. Press and hold the Home button and connect the iPad to the USB cable. Continue to hold until you get a Connect to iTunes screen.

4. Release the Home button and open iTunes. You should see a message that it is in recovery mode. All your content on the iPad will be erased but once it has been recovered you can restore your settings from a previous backup in the normal way.

## Hot Tip

Help! Can't find a new app? There's room on your iPad for 11 pages – Home Screens – full of apps. After that the apps will be there but the only way of finding them is to use Spotlight and search by name. Longer term, think of rearranging your apps in folders.

**Above:** Search for lost apps using the Spotlight bar which can be found by swiping to the right of your Home Screens.

# POWER

You can do so much with your iPad, but as you do more, you do put pressure on the battery. There are ways to conserve power, so you have the energy you need.

## Charging Tips

With early versions of the iPad you could plug the device in and use it while it recharged. Since the third generation iPad, this makes the recharge several hours longer.

> ## Hot Tip
>
> **Strangely, fully charging your iPad and then using it until the power's right down is a good way of improving battery performance. You should try to do this at least once a month.**

- **Recharge the battery**: the best way to recharge the battery is to use the Apple-supplied power adapter to connect the iPad to a power source and turn the device off or put it in sleep mode.

- **Drained battery**: an empty battery doesn't have enough power to show the Home screen, so if your iPad screen is blank when you turn it on, it may have no battery charge. Plug it in and within a few minutes you should see the Charging Please Wait screen. It will be about 10 minutes before there's enough power to see the Home screen.

**Above:** If you see the words Not Charging in your iPad status bar it may be that you are unsuccessfully trying to charge via USB.

- **iPad USB connector**: only use the iPad USB connector, although others, such as the one for the iPhone, look similar, they are not powerful enough to charge the iPad.

- **Not Charging**: you may see the message Not Charging on the iPad status bar, typically, this is when you're trying to charge the iPad through the USB port on your computer. Some older machines don't supply enough power to charge the iPad this way.

○ **Battery percentage indicator:** turn this on so you can see how much charge you have left. Tap Settings, General, Usage, then turn on Battery Percentage.

○ **Usage:** see usage since your last full charge by tapping Settings, General then Usage. The top figure shows how long you've been using the iPad in hours and minutes, the Standby figure indicates how long the iPad has spent in Sleep mode.

## Saving Power

Some features consume more battery power than others and you can conserve energy by turning them off when they're not in use.

○ **Sleep mode:** is the ultimate way of saving power when the iPad is not in use. Activate it by pressing the Sleep/Wake button at the top of the iPad.

○ **Alter screen brightness:** tap Settings, then Brightness & Wallpaper and move the slider to the left.

○ **Turn off Wi-Fi and Cellular:** as your iPad will always try to maintain a connection to a network, you may want to turn these off when you're in areas with low or limited coverage. Go to Settings, Wi-Fi and turn Wi-Fi off. For mobile go to Settings, Cellular and turn off Cellular Data.

○ **Minimize location services:** such as Maps, which can rapidly reduce battery

**Above:** Turning off location services you are not using will make your iPad battery last for longer.

life. Go to Settings, Privacy and turn off the Location Services you don't want.

○ **Switch off push notifications**: some apps are constantly checking when new data is available and will send an alert – push notification – when it is. To disable this, go to Settings, Notifications and turn off Notifications. Similarly, turn off Push Mail when you don't need it or don't want to be disturbed by it. Go to Settings, Mail, Contacts, Calendars, Fetch New Data and set Push to off.

**Above:** Turn off Push mail notifications and change the Fetch frequency to Manually to stop the app gathering new data so often, thus saving battery.

○ **Fetch data less frequently**: instead of having them push new messages to you, you can get applications such as Mail to fetch new data wirelessly after a specific time interval. The shorter the interval, the more frequently data is fetched and the quicker the drain on your battery. Save power by turning this to Manual – Settings, Mail, Contacts, Calendars, Fetch New Data and tap Manually – or setting the Fetch period to a longer time interval, such as hourly.

## Hot Tip
While you can lower screen brightness through the Settings app as above, iBooks has its own brightness control which lets you dim the screen even more.

# RUNNING OUT OF SPACE

Even at 64GB the larger capacity iPads don't offer much storage space compared with a computer. With new apps doing more, they are becoming larger and it's very easy to fill the available space on your iPad quickly.

## Managing Storage Space

If you are running low on storage, there's a quick way of finding out what apps are using the most space, so you can delete those you don't use often.

1.  Tap Settings, then General and Usage. It may take a little time, while it does the calculations, but eventually the iPad lists the top 10 apps that take the most space. Tap an individual app, such as Videos, and you'll get a breakdown of the size occupied by TV series plus individual movies and clips.

2.  Some apps have associated documents and data that also take up space. Tap iMovie and you'll see the total amount of space this takes up (575 MB) is broken down into the size of the app itself (519 MB) and the extra files it has created (56.4 MB in this example).

**Above:** You can check how much storage space individual apps are taking up by tapping Settings, then General and selecting Usage. you may want to free up space by deleting those apps which you don't use very often.

3.  Tap the Usage button to return to the previous screen and then Show all Apps to see a full list of the size of each app. The more apps you have, the longer it takes to build the list.

4.  With the information in front of you, it's easier to clear some space. You can delete the biggest apps you don't use any more or want to remove temporarily: tap on the app then press the Delete App button.

## Hot Tip

Not all apps can be deleted, including those built into iOS, such as the Photos & Camera app or the Music app, which fortunately means you can't accidentally delete all your photos or songs.

# ACCESSORIZING

There are accessories for your iPad that enhance its look, protect it from everyday knocks or, like the wireless keyboard, extend the way it works to make it even easier to use.

## COVERS

From the colourful and zany to the highly functional smart covers, there's plenty of choice when it comes to cases for your iPad. Search online if you are interested in purchasing any of the accessories that follow.

### Smart Cover

Through a series of magnets Apple's smart cover sticks to the side of the iPad. Another set of magnets attach it to the screen, so that opening the cover wakes up the device and closing it puts the iPad to sleep. Inside the micro-fibre surface helps keep the screen clean. The cover also folds into a triangle to create a small stand for the iPad. This is suitable for the iPad 2 and above.

### Leather Portfolio

Go eco-friendly but stay smart with these recycled leather cases for the iPad, which also double as stands. Find the Proporta Recycled Leather Eco Case at www.proporta.com/smart.

### Paper Sleeve

What makes this different is the fact that you can

**Above:** The Papernomad iPad sleeve.

doodle your own designs on the tear-resistant paper cover, while the inside cushioning of cotton and wool protects the iPad. Find the sleeve at www.papernomad.com.

### BookBook
Should you want to disguise the ultimate modern tablet as a vintage book, these leather hardback cases are for you. Doubling up as a typing and display stand, it's available for the iPad 2, 3, 4 and mini.

# STANDS
If you don't want to cover up the elegance of the iPad itself, go for a stand which lets you view the screen hands-free, even watch videos in bed or attach it to a microphone stand for making a speech or presentation.

### PadFoot
A remarkably simple but stylish idea, the PadFoot just clips to the corner of your iPad. It can be used in both landscape and portrait mode. Small enough to be carried easily, it's convenient for use with a wireless keyboard, or standing up the iPad for in-store displays and meeting presentations. Find the PadFoot at www.michielcornelissen.com/padfoot_stand_for_ipad.html.

### Hover Bar
This attaches to any iMac or Apple Display with an L-shaped desk stand and lets you have your iPad beside the big screen, so you can keep an eye on Twitter, the weather or have a FaceTime chat. If you don't have a Mac, the simple silicone-lined clamp makes it easy to set up the

**Left:** The PadFoot clips to the corner of your iPad and keeps it upright without you having to hold it.

iPad for viewing in the kitchen or other room. Find the Hover Bar at www.twelvesouth.com.

## Swingholder

This is designed to keep the iPad at eye-level, whether you're on a treadmill in the gym, lying down in bed or standing on a stage. Based on a microphone stand, it has a weighted base and adjustable swing arm. It works with the iPad 1, 2, 3 and 4 but is relatively expensive. Find the Swingholder on Amazon.

> # Hot Tip
> If you're working on the iPad for a while – watching a movie or playing a game – it can get quite hot, so use a stand or place it on a magazine or tray if you have it on your lap.

# SOUND

Share the music on your iPad at a family get together or in the office by streaming it wirelessly to an external speaker or listen through your headphones to songs playing on the iPad in your backpack.

## Wireless Speakers

As portable as your iPad, the JBL Flip can stream music wirelessly from any Bluetooth-equipped iPad, while the more expensive Bose SoundLink uses Apple's wireless technology AirPlay for what the manufacturers state is clear, room-filling music. Find these speakers at the Apple Store.

**Right:** The JBL flip speakers can be used to wirelessly stream music from your iPad if the Bluetooth is enabled.

## Headphones

No wires needed with Bluetooth-connected headphones, like these ones from Logitech. As most manufacturers offer Bluetooth-enabled headsets that would work with the iPad, make your choice on comfort, sound quality and reliability. Find these headphones at the Apple Store.

# INPUTS

While the iPad's touch screen is great for writing email and such, for longer pieces of text a proper keyboard is much faster and more convenient. And if you want more precise handwritten text or drawings, there are iPad pens to help.

**Above:** The Logitech UE headphones are Bluetooth-enabled, allowing for easy wireless access to the music stored on your iPad.

## Keyboard Stand

This dock has a keyboard physically attached, so you can type – as well as sync, charge and more. Special keys provide quick access to iPad features you use often, such as the Home screen, search and the screen lock. Find the keyboard dock at stores, including John Lewis.

It works with iPad 1, 2, 3 only but not with iPad 4 and mini, as they have the new Lightning connection.

## Bluetooth Keyboard

Bluetooth is a short-range wireless technology that will connect two devices up to about 30 feet away. Because it doesn't need a line of sight connection, it works well with headsets, speakers and particularly keyboards. A Bluetooth enabled keyboard offers much greater freedom, as you can set up and type wherever you are, whether it's on a train or from the comfort of the sofa.

- ○ **Apple**: offer their own wireless keyboard, which will work with Macs as well. Slim and compact, it takes up about a quarter less space than the normal full-sized keyboard. Battery-powered, it will switch off automatically to save power when you're not using the keyboard and then restart instantly when you start typing again. Find the keyboard at the Apple Store.

**Above:** The iPad Keyboard acts as both a dock for your iPad and a battery-powered wireless keyboard.

○ **Kensington**: are among several manufacturers who provide the ultimate iPad travel pack with a case that doubles as a stand and a Bluetooth-enabled keyboard. There are compatible versions available for each iPad generation. Find the keyboard and folio case at www.kensington.com.

## Stylus

One stylus you're not likely to lose grip of is the Cosmonaut. Crayon-sized, with a large rubber barrel, it's more like a marker pen in feel and is great for sketching out ideas or doodling when you need the precision your finger can't offer. Find the Cosmonaut at www.studioneat.com.

## Hot Tip
**Extend the usefulness of your iPad's cameras with Photojojo's fish eye, wide angle and telephoto lenses that attach by a magnetic ring (photojojo.com).**

**Above:** Kensington Bluetooth-enabled keyboard and folio case.

# SECURITY

Given the range of all that you can do on the iPad, from your accounts to buying and selling on the web, there are a number of security measures that can help you keep your private information confidential.

## PASSWORD PROTECTION

The simplest way of keeping your information private is to use password protection – but there are varying degrees of security to the passcodes you use.

### Locking Your iPad – Step-by-Step

1.  Go to Settings, then tap General from the list on the left and scroll down to Passcode Lock. If you turn Simple Passcode on, your password will be a four-digit number. Otherwise, you can use a longer password, featuring numbers and letters, for extra security.

2.  Tap Turn Passcode On. With the Simple Passcode option enter a four-digit number you'll remember and re-enter it when prompted.

3.  Select Require Passcode and select the interval, from more than four hours to immediately, before the iPad locks. The shorter the interval, the more secure it is.

4.  Even when the iPad is locked, there may be certain services you want to use, such as asking Siri to set a Reminder.

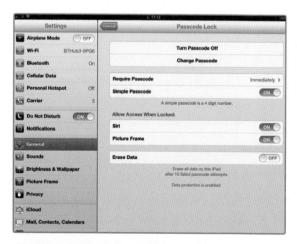

**Above:** Turn on the passcode option within the general settings menu to increase iPad security.

Under the Allow Access When Locked section, choose which apps you want to be available in the background.

5.  If you turn on Erase Data, all information on your iPad is wiped clean after 10 failed attempts to enter the right passcode.

## Auto-Lock

You can automatically lock your iPad or turn off the display when it's not in use. Go to Settings, General then Auto-Lock and select the time delay before it switches off, which varies from 15 minutes to 2 minutes. Set to Never if you don't want the iPad to turn off.

## Cover Locks

The smart covers available on second generation iPads and later will automatically lock your device when you close the cover and turn it back on when you open the flap.

## Encrypting iPad Backups

If you choose this option, passwords for different accounts, such as Mail, will be stored and you won't need to re-enter them individually if you have to use the backup to restore the iPad. Instead, there's one master password you need to restore the backup. To encrypt your backups go to iTunes, select the iPad from the top menu bar, then the Summary tab and check Encrypt iPad Backup.

# Hot Tip

You can also lock the iPad or turn off the display manually, at any time, by pressing the Wake/Sleep button at the top of the iPad.

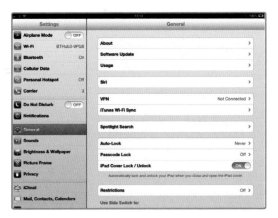

**Above:** Turn on Smart Cover lock to automatically lock your iPad when you close the cover, and turn it back on when you open it.

## iCloud Security

When your personal information is sent from your iPad to iCloud over the internet, it is encrypted, employing the same level of security as that used by major banks. It is also stored on Apple's servers in an encrypted format. That way, your data is kept private and protected from unauthorized access while it's being transmitted to your iPad and when it's stored on iCloud. Apple also recommend you use a strong password with your Apple ID that is used for accessing iCloud. It should be a minimum of eight characters and include uppercase and lowercase letters, and a number.

# FIND MY iPAD

Whether your iPad has been stolen or you've simply mislaid it, you can track it down, provided you've already set up Find My iPad.

## Find Your Device

1. To start tracking of your iPad, go to Settings, iCloud and turn on Find My iPad.

2. As soon as you've done this, a permission box opens, asking you to confirm you are happy for the iPad to be tracked and its location shown on a map. Tap Allow.

**Above:** Turn on Find My iPad in your iCloud settings to ensure it can be tracked via Location Services.

3. In Settings tap Privacy and turn on Location Services. Find My iPad should also be turned on.

4. You can download the Find My iPad app (called Find My iPhone) from iTunes and use this on another iDevice, such as iPhone, to track your iPad. Once it's downloaded, log in using your iCloud username and password.

5. Alternatively, you can log in direct through Find My iPhone on the iCloud website. Go to www.icloud.com and use your Apple ID to sign in. Click on Devices, and any that can be found are shown with a green pin on the map. Any that can't be located will have a red pin.

6. Click on the pin, and it shows you the last time the iPad was tracked to that address. Click on the information button and a new window opens.

Other features of Find My iPad include:

**Above**: You can choose actions for when your iPad has been tracked, for example playing sounds, locking it remotely and erasing its content.

○ **Play Sound**: sends a strange bell-clanging noise to your iPad – handy if you know it's in your home somewhere, but you have misplaced it.

○ **Lost mode**: lets you lock your iPad remotely, with a four-digit passcode if you haven't set one already, which is useful if you've left it at work or a friend's house.

○ **Erase iPad**: the nuclear option if you believe it has been stolen, this wipes out all the iPad's content, including your private, sensitive information and restores the device to the original factory settings.

## LIMITING ACCESS

If you don't want every user to have full reign over your iPad, such as a business colleague

### Hot Tip

For Find My iPad to work, it has to be turned on at all times, which will use some battery power, but it does offer great peace of mind in case anything happens to your iPad.

or your children, you can limit the areas they can access.

## Setting Restrictions

In order to set up the rules of who can access what, tap Settings, General, Restrictions then Enable Restrictions. In the pop-up window set a passcode and re-enter to confirm.

**Above:** Set up restrictions to limit access to parts of your iPad.

- **Restrict Apps**: If you turn off any of the apps listed here – which include Safari, Camera and apps that use it, FaceTime, iTunes Store, iBookstore and Siri – they can only be used by someone who knows the password.

- **Disable Installing of Apps**: the App Store is also disabled and its icon is removed from the Home screen. Alternatively, if you keep the App Store accessible, you can prevent your children from adding expensive extras to apps by turning off In-App Purchases or Require a Password before they can buy.

- **Prevent Deleting of Apps**: by removing the delete icon (x) from the corner of apps.

- **Avoid Explicit Language**: with Siri using asterisks and beep sounds to cover any unfortunate words that may slip out during dictation.

- **Lock your accounts**: including your current Mail, Contacts, Calendar and iCloud settings.

- **Set Content Restrictions**: for music and podcasts, books, movies, TV shows, and apps, according to the country you select from the list. Any content outside of the ratings you select won't be shown on the iPad.

**Above**: Turn on Guided Access to use kiosk mode to limit your iPad to a single app when needed.

## Guided Access

If you want to share a single presentation, use your iPad solely as a photo frame during a party or have your child focus on a single game, then you can use kiosk mode. This limits the iPad to a single app, with you controlling what features are available.

Tap Settings, then General, Accessibility, Guided Access and slide the button to On. Set a passcode to use. Select the app you want to use, triple-press the Home button, adjust the settings and press Start.

# PRIVACY SETTINGS

You can control which apps have access to your personal information in your contacts, calendars, reminders and photos, as well as Twitter and Facebook.

## Controlling Access

The first time an app tries to access your personal information, a pop-up box will ask if you allow this or not. Whatever your response, the decision stands and the app won't ask again. However, you can change your mind.

To change your privacy choice, go to Settings, Privacy and select one of the apps from the list, for example Contacts. Here you'll see a list of apps, such as Skype or Find Friends, that have asked to access this personal information. You can allow or disallow access by switching the button to On or Off.

### Hot Tip

If you want to wipe the slate clean and start again, you can reset all your privacy warnings. Go to Settings, General, Reset and tap Reset Location & Privacy.

**Above:** Activate the Limit Ad Tracking setting to prevent online advertisers from using your web data to target you specifically.

## Stop Ad Tracking

This is a new privacy setting added to iOS 6 that prevents advertisers using your web usage data and cookies (which have information about the sites you visit) to target specific ads to you.

To turn it on go to Settings, General, About and scroll down to Advertising, then turn on Limit Ad Tracking.

## Fraud Warning

Go to Settings, Safari and scroll down to turn this on. This checks websites you visit against a public database of problem sites. If you follow a link to one of these sites, you get a warning, so you can stop loading the page.

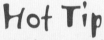

## Hot Tip

You can have more than one VPN connection and switch between them on the VPN settings page. A VPN button appears in the status bar when you're using the secure connection.

## VPN

Connect securely and privately to your office network, via the internet, using a virtual private network (VPN).

### Setting up a VPN Connection

Go to the Settings app, select General then VPN and slide the button to On.

In the window that opens enter your network settings, which you will need to get from your IT department (or copy from your Mac or PC if you already have a VPN set up on your computer). When complete, tap Save.

# APPTASTIC: 100 BEST iPAD APPS

There are more than a quarter of a million apps designed exclusively for the iPad in the App Store. Many are brilliant, some not so. Here, in line with the different categories covered in this book, is our pick of the essential apps (excluding built-in apps) for a fantastic iPad experience.

## Communication

1. **Facebook**: The official app for the world's largest social network.

2. **Friendly for Facebook**: The full Facebook experience designed specifically for the iPad.

3. **Twitter**: All you need to go a-tweeting.

4. **Tweetbot**: Nice design and lots of ways to customize your Twitter experience.

5. **LinkedIn**: Keep in touch with your professional network.

6. **HootSuite for Twitter and Facebook**: Manage several of your social networks from one app.

7. **StumbleUpon**: Stumble your way through a creative network of videos, photos and web pages.

8. **Skype for iPad**: Instant message, voice or video call to friends and family around the world.

9. **Find My Friends**: Stalk your friends and family.

10. **Google Maps**: Once powered the built-in Maps app but now there's only this iPhone version for the iPad.

## Connectivity

11. **iTap VNC (Remote Desktop for Windows and Mac)**: Manage your desktop from your iPad.

## Photos

12. **Guardian Eyewitness**: Daily showcase of some of the most striking and beautiful photographs.

13. **iPhoto**: Browse, edit and share your photos from the iPad.

14. **Adobe Photoshop Touch**: Tablet-designed version of the famous photo-editing software.

15. **Snapseed**: Makes pro-level photo-editing easy.

16. **Brushes 3**: The painting app that's so good that artist David Hockney uses it.

17. **Instagram**: iPhone version of the fun social network for taking and sharing photos.

18. **Instant**: Polaroid instant photos for the iPad.

19. **ComicBook**: Fully featured app for creating comic books.

20. **PhotoSync**: Wirelessly transfers your photos and videos.

21. **Web Albums HD for Picasa and Google+**: Viewer and photo manager for the online photo services.

22. **FlickStackr**: Lets you browse, upload and share photos on Flickr.

23. **eBook Magic**: The app for creating and sharing many types of book.

24. **Greetings Studio**: Easy-to-use greeting card app for the iPad.

25. **InstaCalendar for iPad**: Convenient way of using your photos to create a calendar.

26. **Jigsawed Jigsaw Puzzle**: Easily customizable jigsaw puzzle creator.

## TV, Movies and Music Video

27. **YouTube**: No longer a built-in app, but you can still get access to one of the world's greatest collections of videos.

28. **Vimeo**: Designed for watching, creating and sharing videos on the Vimeo site.

29. **iMovie**: Movie-editing for the touchscreen.

30. **Skyfire Web Browser for iPad**: The browser that does let you watch Flash videos on the iPad.

31. **Netflix**: The subscription service for watching TV and films on your iPad.

32. **Matcha – Find and Watch Movies & TV**: Personalized guide for video services.

33. **Plizy**: Discover the best movies, shows and web content online.

34. **Crackle – Movies & TV**: Watch free Hollywood movies and TV shows.

35. **BBC iPlayer**: Watch and listen to BBC TV and Radio.

## Books/News

36. **iBooks**: Apple's ebook reader and bookstore.

37. **Google Play Books**: Provides access to millions of books – free and paid-for.

38. **Kindle**: Reader for Kindle books, newspapers, magazines and more from the Amazon store.

39. **Newsweek**: Digital editions especially created for the iPad.

40. **The *Guardian* and *Observer* iPad edition**: The newspapers re-imagined for the iPad.

41. ***MailOnline* for iPad**: Standalone app with customizable international editions linked to the UK's number one newspaper website.

42. **BBC News**: Breaking news from around the world.

43. **Reuters News Pro for iPad**: Professional-grade news and market data.

44. **Early Edition 2**: Edit your own newspaper.

45. **NewsRack**: Fully featured news reader.

46. **Flipboard: Your Social News Magazine**: Personal magazine combining international news sources and your social networks.

47. **Pocket**: Lets you save content from the web to read later.

48. **ESPN ScoreCenter**: Results and news from sports leagues around the world.

49. **Zinio**: Buy and read magazines on your iPad.

50. **Zite**: Personalized magazine that learns what you like.

51. **Comics**: Read comics on your iPad.

52. **Dilbert Mobile**: Animated cartoons on office life.

## Reference/Lifestyle

53. **Shakespeare**: The complete works.

54. **Encyclopaedia Britannica**: If you don't trust free encyclopedias, this offers a rolling monthly subscription to one of the most respected reference sources.

55. **Wikipanion**: If you do trust free encyclopedias, this is a faster and easier way to access Wikipedia.

56. **Google Earth**: Fly around the planet from your iPad.

57. **World Atlas HD**: World maps designed specifically to display on the iPad.

58. **Weather**: Is it cold outside? Find out.

59. **HowStuffWorks for iPad**: All you need to know.

60. **NASA App HD**: Explore the universe from your iPad.

61. **National Geographic Magazine-International**: The magazine plus special interactive content.

62. **WebMD**: Health information and symptom checker for the hypochondriac in you.

63. **Epicurious**: Recipes for foodies.

64. **TripAdvisor Hotels Flights Restaurants**: Candid reviews by fellow travellers.

65. **TripDeck**: When you've decided where you're going, this is your itinerary organizer. iPhone app.

66. **Fancy**: Explore and buy from a crowd-created catalogue of amazing gifts and goodies.

## Entertainment

67. **Podcasts**: Manage your podcasts.

68. **Spotify**: Access millions of songs and listen free or subscribe.

69. **Last.fm**: iPhone app for access to the music recommendation site from your iPad.

70. **Vevo HD**: High-quality music videos.

71. **TuneIn Radio Pro**: Listen to and record music, sports and news radio around the world.

72. **SoundHound**: Fast music recognition app.

73. **Amazon Cloud Player**: iPhone app for listening to your music stored on the Amazon Cloud.

74. **GarageBand**. Your own recording studio.

75. **Angry Birds**: Destroy greedy pigs in a number of environments.

76. **The Dark Knight Rises**: Game inspired by the movie.

77. **Tiger Woods PGA Tour**: Life as a golf pro.

78. **Scrabble**: The word game designed just for the iPad.

79. **We Rule Deluxe for iPad**: The longest-running social game on iDevices.

## Work

80. **GoodReader for iPad**: Robust, flexible PDF reader.

81. **Dictionary.com**: English dictionary and thesaurus for the iPad.

82. **Evernote**: Sync notes, to-do lists, documents, photos and more across all your devices.

83. **Dropbox**: Share and sync your docs, photos and videos.

84. **Things for iPad**: Easy-to-use task manager.

85. **OmniFocus for iPad**: Fully featured organizer for a busy life.

86. **Pages**: Word-processor app for the iPad.

87. **Numbers**: Spreadsheet app for the iPad.

88. **Keynote**: Presentation app for the iPad.

89. **Quickoffice Pro HD**: Edit Microsoft Office documents and view PDF files.

90. **Google Drive**: Create, share and keep all your documents online in one place.

91. **SugarSync**: Online backup, mobile syncing and file sharing.

92. **Blogsy for iPad**: Blog writing for the iPad.

93. **iTranslate**: Translate words and texts into 50 languages.

94. **PrintCentral Pro**: Print to all printers (not just AirPrint printers).

95. **Bento 4 for iPad**: Personal database for organizing contacts, tracking projects and managing lists.

96. **SharePrice**: Track your investments across global markets.

97. **Account Tracker**: Powerful personal finance app.

98. **Countdown Timer Pro**: Build up the anticipation, or anxiety, and count down to any date.

## Security

99. **1Password**: Remember the master password and 1Password remembers the rest.

100. **Find My iPhone**: Use another iDevice to find your iPad and protect your data.

# INDEX